Encouraging Civility as a Community College Leader

Edited by Paul A. Elsner
and George R. Boggs

Community College Press®
a division of the American Association of Community Colleges
Washington, DC

2005

The American Association of Community Colleges (AACC) is the primary advocacy organization for the nation's community colleges. The association represents more than 1,100 two-year, associate degree-granting institutions and more than 11 million students. AACC promotes community colleges through six strategic action areas: national and international recognition and advocacy, learning and accountability, leadership development, economic and workforce development, connectedness across AACC membership, and international and intercultural education. Information about AACC and community colleges may be found at www.aacc.nche.edu.

Design: Grace Design, LLC
Editors: Donna Carey and Deanna D'Errico
Printer: Kirby Lithographic

© 2005 American Association of Community Colleges

Community College Press
American Association of Community Colleges
One Dupont Circle, NW
Suite 410
Washington, DC 20036

Printed in the United States of America.

ISBN 0-87117-362-X

Contents

Foreword

Civility can be an emotionally loaded word—conjuring up images of a table with too much silverware—however, civility is a truly democratic word, sharing roots with the terms civil, civic, and *civilized*. Civility is a civic virtue commonly associated with politeness, good manners, and rectitude, but it is also an ethical principle that promotes respect for people and thus is a foundation of the civil state. Rather than a prescription for behavior, civility embodies a sense of the ethical underpinnings of social relations and mutual respect in discourse. Because I believe that civility is embedded in ethics and in civic participation, as well as human communication, over the past decade I have examined a variety of fields to unfurl a notion of civility for the community college classroom.

My interest in civility and etiquette began in my childhood, when my aunt and I had tea parties—strategically designed to teach me manners. Later I observed that some people used etiquette in a harmful, exclusionary way to exhibit supposedly superior knowledge. Etiquette was used, beginning in the early 1900s, to accentuate classes of Americans within society. In fact, the proliferation of types of forks and their placement on the table was more about acquiring arcane, exclusionary knowledge than acquiring or using silverware. Etiquette can still cloak with false sweetness the cudgel of discrimination. I wanted to understand the distinctions between etiquette, a codified set of manners, and civility, the underlying respect for "other." Later, when I taught leadership as a part of student government, I wanted to convey the importance of respect and trust as key factors in leadership and cooperation:

> Decrying lack of civility is cyclical, beginning with Aristotle (circa 399 BC). Children today love luxury too much. They have detestable manners, flout authority, and have no respect for their elders. They no longer rise when their parents and teachers enter the room. What kind of awful creatures will they be when they grow up?

The most recent hue and cry began in the popular media in the mid-1990s when the term *incivility* appeared in the headlines. Although in the late 1990s, secondary education addressed the issue as "character education," little has been written at the community college level. Recent interest, however, is evident: The Accrediting Commission for Community and Junior Colleges (AACJC) has incorporated the concepts of civility and interpersonal skills into accreditation (2004).

This important book provides a personal glimpse into the experiences of pragmatic community college leaders who have grappled with conflict, sometimes in the absence of civility. These authors have asked, "What happens when civility breaks down?" They have described incivility in many forms, including matters of race, ethnicity, gender, sexual preference, and physical abilities. The chapters here provide a history and context for the theoretical concepts of leadership, respect, and trust—all essential factors in the promulgation of civility.

The most important ideas from these chapters are the lessons learned by leaders across the nation about modeling civility, reminders of shared goals, importance of staff development and support, and the value of diversity. In many instances, the contributors have recommended ways to increase civility on campus, setting a tone for the college community as one of mutual respect and civil discourse.

A college environment can encourage civility to give students opportunities for construction of knowledge (content) as well as developing skills essential for social interaction (process) as citizens in the community. Fostering such a learning environment should be the responsibility of everyone on campus. In an ideal classroom setting, a diverse group of participants express a range of views. The instructor sets forth explicit expectations of mutual respect and civil discourse, and fosters discussions among class members about the relevance of civility, respect, and discourse. Open discussion helps students practice critical thinking skills, as they learn to be open to the ideas of others, rather than to simply defend their own ideas.

Outside the classroom, opportunities to engage in experienced-based learning, as well as campus and community-based activities such as service learning are vital. Students should be encouraged to participate in leadership development and in governance of the college. Colleges should promote and offer events and speakers in an environment that challenges thinking and opinions. Colleges should support community mentorships for students and faculty mentorships for new faculty. Recognition of contributions to campus and community should be frequent and public.

Responsibility in instruction goes beyond imparting content. The instructor models respect for learning and respect for participants in the learning process; he or she encourages discussion that is mutually respectful and open to and tolerant of other views. This is equally true for both math and English classes, for laser technology and guidance.

Judy Rookstool
Coordinator, Teaching and Learning
Evergreen Valley College

References

Accrediting Commission for Community and Junior Colleges, Western Association of Schools and Colleges. (2004). *Accreditation standards II*. Available from www.accjc.org

Preface

This book presents the experiences and points of view of community college presidents and chancellors who have undergone challenging transformations and adaptations to intense political and social upheavals. The contributors value their experiences as leaders in difficult and challenging contexts, and most feel that they achieved success even in less-than-civil environments.

The book calls for a deeper dialogue on the importance of civility in what community college leaders often refer to as the "academy." We cite examples of our challenges, trials, and even some successes in this environment, and the book has helped us recall and collate some defining experiences in our careers. Although the book is presented mainly from an administrative perspective, it does not intend to omit or minimize the challenges and frustrations that faculty and staff may experience as a result of working in uncivil settings.

The contributors relate examples of situations in which we encountered unexpected and sometimes unprecedented incivility in our role as community college leaders. The chapters present our experiences, observations, lessons, and recommendations for handling crises that may befall leaders in an academic setting. Sometimes these crises seem only tangentially related to the core mission of the colleges: serving students and communities. Yet these situations arise and must be dealt with in order for the colleges to survive and continue that mission. Through these examples we hope to advance strategies and stimulate further ideas for maintaining and encouraging an atmosphere of civility despite acrimonious and even hostile conditions that may arise on a college campus or in a college's surrounding community.

In chapter 1, editor and contributor Paul Elsner relates some of the tumultuous events that occurred during his tenure at Peralta Community College District in California in the 1960s and as chancellor of the Maricopa County Community College District in Arizona. Elsner presents examples of breakdowns in civility that can occur in the academic setting and hopes to send the message that even in the worst times of stress and turmoil, leaders are not alone; they share similar challenges with many other colleges and colleagues.

In chapter 2, Martha Gandert Romero provides a model for how a CEO can survive an orchestrated, ideological community attack. She offers the sound advice that the time to make friends in the community is before, not during, a crisis. Leaders need to build a base of trust and support both on campus and in the community long before that support may be needed. People on campus can see when a leader is respected in the community, making the leader less vulnerable to unreasonable internal or external attacks.

In chapter 3, Beverly Simone reminds leaders that unless the college is new, the organization has a culture that existed long before the current leaders joined the college. Nonetheless, each of us has the power to affect the environment and to set a model for the kind of behavior that our institutions, our students, our faculty and staff, and our communities deserve. Simone discusses a circumstance in which board members were not willing to prohibit bullying behavior on the part of her board chair, and she presents some of the positive strategies she was able to institute to encourage campus civility.

In chapter 4, Zelema Harris points out that even top administrators may be guilty of using incivility as a strategy. Some may purposefully try to intimidate people in order to keep problems from emerging and becoming visible. Perhaps they are unsure of their leadership ability and believe that, if problems are unreported, they can deny their existence and not have to address them. Harris believes that the CEO must change or remove these kinds of administrators in order to improve the long-term climate of the institution. Her experience is that a CEO can expect bottled-up problems to surface when the threat is removed, but the climate will eventually improve as a more trusting environment emerges.

In chapter 5, Paul Elsner suggests several causes of incivility on campus and presents perspectives on the preservation of freedom of speech and attempts to institute speech codes. The chapter includes a transcript from a candid interview with an associate dean from the University of California at Irvine regarding the challenges to civility on college campuses. Finally, the chapter offers recommendations for leaders to consider for anticipating problem situations and encouraging campus civility.

Community colleges are often referred to as the colleges of democracy. Our institutions should be models of civil discourse—respecting people, allowing all to have their say, but supporting legitimate governance authority. How educators, leaders, and policymakers behave sets a tone for behavior of others even beyond our campuses. Moreover, once a climate and patterns of behavior are set on a campus, they are difficult to change. New employees, students, and leaders enter an environment that has been created by those who came before. Trustees, leaders, and faculty members have an opportunity to improve the learning and working environments on their campuses by making them more civil places.

Paul A. Elsner
Chancellor Emeritus, Maricopa County Community College District
President and Founder, Sedona Conferences and Conversations

George R. Boggs
President and Chief Executive Officer
American Association of Community Colleges

Civility on Campus

George R. Boggs

"No college can survive unless its members are willing to respect and attempt to grasp the ideas, thoughts, opinions, theories, sensibilities, and feelings of others. In this sharing, we keep an open mind; we suspend our final judgment, we tolerate the new, the strange, the disconcerting, the troubling, the at least temporarily unknown or unresolved. We respond in the full expectation that our listeners, in turn, will meet with respect our own original or modified notions and points of view. If this sharing does not occur, no new knowledge is developed, nor do our minds continue to grow." —Statement on Tolerance, State University of New York

People who have chosen careers in community colleges are fortunate in many ways. Community colleges make it possible for people to learn and to realize their dreams for a better future. Community colleges allow flexible work schedules, often provide an attractive work environment on college campuses or education centers, and afford the opportunity to work with intelligent and highly motivated colleagues. Most of us have the impression that there is a consistently high level of public respect for community college educators and leaders. This impression springs from news stories, supportive editorials, and general public testimony that we as leaders often see and hear.

Many students would not have an opportunity to attend college if not for community colleges. The American Association of Community Colleges has received reports of countless stories of students who have benefited from the nurturing environment in community colleges and who have gone on to successful careers and lives. Community colleges make it possible for students to achieve their educational goals and to improve their lives and those of their families.

Yet, despite these seeming advantages, stories also surface about how poorly college employees treat one another in our institutions. Those who have been involved in community college education for long enough will have witnessed poor treatment of students, disruptive behaviors on the part of students, mean-spirited behavior among colleagues in department or committee meetings, lack of respect for classified support staff, hostility between administrators and faculty, and dysfunctional boards of trustees that set a tone for incivility. At the very least, these behaviors detract from the positive work that educators do for students and communities. In some cases, incivility on campuses even leads to health problems and threats of violence. At the extreme, some college leaders have had to employ security guards for themselves and their families and even, in at least one case, to work behind a bulletproof shield.

A long-term college president told me about a bitter experience she had in her first presidency. At first she thought the position was a perfect fit and began with the expected high level of enthusiasm. It soon became apparent, however, that there were a few employees whose poor behavior had long been accepted by the leadership. The employees enjoyed their own power base and viewed their uncivil behavior as entertainment. These individuals expressed their displeasure with the new president through threatening phone calls and by sneaking a dead animal onto her car.

As Paul Elsner observes, it is possible that some angry and thoughtless people may not want a civil setting and may even derive a sense of reward from the divisiveness they engender. This observation reminded me of a conversation I had with a faculty member early in my tenure as a new community college president. I observed a bright and articulate faculty member who I believed had the potential to develop into an effective and positive campus leader. It seemed to me, however, that she had a negative attitude and was a disruptive influence. One day over lunch, I asked this faculty member about her behavior. Her response was that the behavior was purposeful and that she believed it was the source of her power. Because others saw that she was bold enough to exhibit negative behavior, she told me, others sought her help with their problems, and she felt valued by them. Although we were able to create a climate in which people felt safe in addressing their concerns though regular college processes, this woman did not significantly change her behavior and did not progress to a more responsible leadership role.

Sometimes, rude behavior may not even be noticed by those who exhibit it. Students who are continually late for class and employees who are perpetually late for meetings and appointments may not recognize this behavior as an act of incivility. The same might be said of those who allow pagers and cell phones to interrupt a class, a conference presentation, or a meeting. Even those who engage in more serious acts of incivility may not recognize how disruptive they are. If they do, they may feel their behavior is justified.

Possible Causes of Incivility

Community colleges are socially embedded institutions. As such, our colleges are affected by behaviors in the larger society. Although there may be some disagreement about whether society in general is becoming less civil, examples can be found on talk radio shows, television shows, political advertisements, and even in the press, where people are often personally attack each other rather than debate their ideas. As educators, we should understand our role in shaping societal values rather than just emulating them. Community college campuses should be models of civil and respectful environments. In particular, colleges can inform new students about codes of conduct and expectations for their behavior. These same values should be communicated to new employees, and codes of ethics should be referenced during orientations. New students and new employees will, however, be influenced more by the behaviors they witness than by what they are told.

Whenever highly intelligent, articulate, and caring people are brought together in one place, as they are on a college campus, one can expect that many different ideas will be generated, and not everyone will agree on the best course of action. This environment is one that can yield a healthy, studied, and respectful discussion of issues and courses of action so that the best decisions are made. On the other hand, bad behavior on the part of a few people can convert this situation into one of distrust and hostility.

Loss of Trust and Respect

A faculty member once told me that he believed incivility between administrators and faculty was due to a loss of trust. Generally, a lack of trust leads to a lack of respect. This faculty member believes that the loss of trust between administrators and faculty stems from the different perspectives they have and the assumptions they make about one another. In other words, he sees this situation as a natural occurrence unless faculty members and administrators work to bridge the gap in perspective and to avoid making incorrect and inappropriate assumptions. In addition, it is all too common on college campuses one sees a lack of respect for classified or support staff. Because of their perceived status, they may not be treated with the same deference that is shown to faculty and academic administrators.

Declining Resources

A retired community college president told me that he believes campus incivility has grown over the years and respect for the role of the president has diminished primarily because resources have declined. While this failing is not discussed in the following chapters, we occasionally hear CEOs link incivility with tight budgets or troubling resource shortages. At the same time that funds lagged behind inflation, faculty members and CEOs were moving up on salary schedules and demanding more for salaries and benefits while criticizing other college expenditures. Colleges do not have the funds to meet everyone's demands.

As evidence that lack of sufficient funding can be a cause of incivility, there are reports of an increasing number of votes of no confidence in the leadership of presidents as they deal with cuts in state funding. College leaders are faced with few alternatives to difficult decisions that affect positions, benefits, and working conditions for employees and tuition costs and available course sections for students. Employees sometimes take their frustrations out on the college leadership.

A recently retired college president told me that she too believed lack of resources to be an important cause for conflict and incivility. Departments compete with other departments, credit programs compete with noncredit programs, student services compete with academic services, transfer programs compete with technical and trade programs. She has seen faculty members, including department chairs, degrade their colleagues in attempts to secure more resources for their areas.

Resistance to Authority

Another community college leader told me he believed "friends may come and go, but enemies accumulate." With every decision a leader makes, there are people on the opposite side. This person made the point that, even if people may be on the leader's side of an issue in the future, they remember times when they were not. Eventually, a critical mass of unhappy people might use uncivil behavior to try to make it impossible for a leader to be effective. People who oppose a leader's decisions may look for ways to bring him or her down.

Because they encourage freedom of expression and thought, college campuses may seem to sanction the questioning of authority. In fact, it could be said that some people on our campuses have an anti-authority philosophy. Academia may value egalitarianism, even to the extent of not wanting to see others recognized for excellence; but even more often, this value conflicts with the acceptance of authority. Although the governance systems of colleges are usually designed for inclusiveness and involvement, the colleges are not democracies, and someone in authority has to be responsible for decisions and their outcomes.

The tension caused by superimposing the authority and responsibility of leadership on campuses that resist it can be a source of incivility.

Tenure laws were designed to protect the academic freedom of faculty members and to allow them to examine controversial subjects and sometimes to express unpopular points of view in their classrooms. These protections also can be effective shields for bad behavior toward students, classified staff, and administrators. Moreover, administrators may be seen as fair game for attack. Colleagues who accept a leadership position place themselves in the line of fire and may lose their right to fair treatment.

Incivility as a Protest Strategy

A long-term president told me of his experience in dealing with elected department chairs after taking on the presidency of a new institution. Because the chairs were elected rather than appointed, they felt they had a mandate to look out for the interests of their departments and their faculty above all else. They felt that administrative performance review was inappropriate because they faced reelection by their peers every three years. According to the president, the department chairs had a history of behaving unprofessionally and sanctioning unprofessional conduct, and using these strategies to get what they felt they needed.

Collective Bargaining

Collective bargaining is a process that can foster bad behavior as a strategy for achieving specific ends. Because they are essentially advocacy organizations, unions have the potential to create an environment in which people feel adversarial and may then feel entitled to behave uncivilly to make their demands known. Sometimes management teams also participate in these negative games of posturing. After the bargaining is concluded, people may expect a situation to go back to the way it was before conflicts took place. Unfortunately, the hurt and damage caused by hostile negotiations may last for years and affect the climate of an institution.

Votes of No Confidence

Votes of no confidence can be examples of a strategic use of incivility. They may be seen by faculty and staff as their only weapons against a poor or intimidating leader; however, there are no consistent rules governing the purpose and use of these votes. Often they are taken in response to stalled salary or contract negotiations rather than poor leadership. They seem to be more common in difficult financial times when leaders are faced with difficult decisions. In the leaders' point of view, it may seem that employees simply need someone to blame for a bad situation, and the leader is the most convenient person to blame.

One CEO described his experience in dealing with a faculty that went on strike to try to secure a 10% pay increase. The president docked nine weeks of pay for those who were involved in the strike. His decision was appealed, but the state Supreme Court found in favor of the president. The faculty responded with a vote of no confidence, although no charges were ever leveled against the president.

Administrative reorganizations are another frequent cause of votes of no confidence. Faculty members often strongly resist changes in how the college is run. The chancellor of a large district told me about one of his college presidents who had restructured her college about seven years earlier, eliminating two vice president positions, combining them to form an executive vice president position. One of the displaced vice presidents became vice president of the faculty association before it voted no confidence in the president's leadership. The chancellor stood behind the decision of the president, however, and believes that the college has become more productive because of her decision.

At one point in my career as a college president, the faculty senate took a vote of no confidence (later changed to a vote of censure) in two of my vice presidents. In my opinion the issue was one of power, as the two vice presidents had acted, with my support, to void a faculty search because of the lack of sufficient size and diversity of the finalist pool. The search committee believed that it had acted in good faith to deliver a single finalist and did not believe that administrators should have the authority to override its selection. The aggrieved search committee took its case to the faculty senate, which acted to punish these two administrators. As president, I defended my administrators before the faculty senate, and the board of trustees and I stood behind the decision of the administration.

Moreover, as Elsner points out, there is little consistency in how these votes are taken. Sometimes only the faculty senate or one of its subcommittees is authorized to take the vote. Even when the vote involves the whole faculty or the faculty and staff, they are not usually briefed on the issues of concern, and the leader almost never has an opportunity to offer a rebuttal or defense before an anonymous vote is taken.

A college president told me that she believed that votes of no confidence have taken on a different meaning than they had when she first entered the profession. The votes no longer signify a lack of integrity, competence, or ethical behavior. Instead, they are a strong protest against any leadership action with which people disagree. The vote no longer carries the significance or weight that it once did.

Confronting Incivility

A long-term president told me of his experience in moving into a new presidency in a different part of the country. At the new college, the president found that unpleasant behavior had been ignored and even sanctioned by leadership. He believed that the previous president had used the incivility in his institution to his advantage to put people in their place. Although this behavior may be unusual, some leaders may not actively encourage bad behavior, but do nothing to discourage it, either.

Leaders have an obligation to confront instances of incivility. As one CEO expressed to me, a leader cannot let it go but must confront it. People can disagree, but they must be professional. No one should be put on the spot without advanced notice. No one, including students, staff, faculty, administrators, or trustees, should be subjected to mean-spirited behavior, and the CEO is often in the best position to say what is unacceptable.

Early in my presidency, I experienced a situation in which board members would publicly embarrass and deride two of my vice presidents. Although I came to believe that the board members were essentially correct in their assessment of these people, I convinced the board members to confine their criticisms of the administration to me. The appropriate forum for commenting on the administration's effectiveness was the CEO's evaluation, not at an open board meeting. Of course, college faculty members or leaders often must act to defend a student or an employee to ensure that he or she is treated with respect and to confront unacceptable behavior. Only if people are willing to do what is right will our institutions reach their full potential by supporting people to be effective learners, employees, leaders, and trustees in a healthy environment.

A well-functioning board of trustees will act in a similar manner to protect its CEO. I recall a case in which a faculty organization presented a vote of no confidence in the president to the chair of the board at a board meeting. The board chair read the statement in silence and then handed it back to the faculty representative, saying that he could not accept it because it did not also list the same degree of no confidence in the board. The message was that the CEO was behaving as the board wished, and the board would not seriously consider the vote.

If the CEO exhibits intimidating behavior, it is the responsibility of the board of trustees or system administrator to take corrective action. The retired executive director of a regional accrediting commission told me that, in his view, some CEOs and other leaders simply do not persons who value civility. Because the makeup of faculty leadership is relatively stable compared with that of boards and CEOs, the chances of an institution having a board member or CEO who offends the faculty is statistically increased.

Some prominent CEOs, in the opinion of this accreditation leader, discount points of view other than their own and, being people of considerable intelligence, have used legal systems and other forms of intimidation to create negative campus environments. In some cases, leaders single out opposition leaders for personal ridicule and defamation. Even after such a CEO leaves a campus, the negative climate and level of distrust may linger.

A chancellor told me of his experience surviving a disruptive board of trustees. Two new board members had personal agendas, unrelated to student learning and the welfare of the colleges. The behavior of these trustees was to disrupt. Many times, the chancellor was given assignments without visible objectives. Sometimes, the assignment was designed to generate data for use in the political campaigns of the board members. The chancellor finally told the board that the district would need to employ at least three new full-time people in the research office to comply with all of their demands. This suggestion stopped the burdensome requests. The last election changed the composition of the board for the better.

An experienced CEO told me that he believed leaders should not be reluctant to confront the people who engage in unprofessional behavior. He thinks it is important to get conflicts out into the open and to do it every time. He advocates the use of convocations to identify unhealthy behavior and to call for better behavior without accusing any individuals. He develops an individualized strategy for offenders, to try to bring them into the mainstream. He has found over the years that many of these negative people can be turned around.

This same experienced CEO recently held a meeting with department chairs and handed out some of the unprofessional materials that were distributed on campus. After some reflection, an influential member of the group told the president that he was right, and the group had a discussion about how it might stop this damaging behavior.

When informal confrontations fail, the leader must be prepared to use formal disciplinary proceedings. A president told me of a problem she experienced with a male faculty member who lashed out at female students and clerks. When the president was unable to persuade the faculty member to change this behavior, she initiated disciplinary proceedings. The agreed on remedy that to included anger management training. At the extreme, the remedy may be termination of employment.

This same CEO who confronted his department chairs told me that he has used a similar strategy to improve board behavior. First, he tries an appeal to the individual trustee who is causing the problem, explicitly telling the trustee what the problem is and why the CEO sees it as a problem. If a pattern of bad behavior develops, the CEO shares copies of any offensive materials with the other board members, sometimes writing an explanation or commentary. His intent is to appeal to the higher instincts of the board and to make it a self-policing, self-correcting body, if possible. Ideally, the board chair should be the person to confront bad board behavior. If this does not happen, however, the CEO may have to be the person to try to improve the behavior and functioning of the board.

Many CEOs have told me that they have seen cases of board members who may have been elected or appointed because of a special interest but who eventually come to understand their responsibilities and become good board members. A long-term chancellor told me of his belief in the importance of treating all board members alike, despite being mistreated by some of them. His advice was not to lash back or to lose your temper. He has found that it is possible to turn bad board members around if they are treated with respect.

For a leader to survive attacks, he or she must understand the behavioral group dynamics of faculty and governing boards. These groups are more likely to provide support to the leader if the attacks are external. Groups seem to be very reluctant to confront unacceptable behavior among their peers. I believe that a leader is more likely to receive this kind of support if the leader is seen as someone who defends others against unacceptable behavior and someone who is fair and honest in dealing with people. Support from the community can strengthen both the external and internal positions of a leader, but the development of community support requires a long-term commitment.

The media often plays an important role in times of crisis. Leaders need to respond appropriately to media requests while respecting the legal necessity for some matters to remain confidential. Leaders always set the tone for their institutions, a fact that is never truer than when a leader is under attack.

Strategies to Improve Campus Civility

Many college leaders have expressed to me the importance of communication for creating and maintaining a civil campus environment. Leaders need to be visible, to listen to people, and to avoid allowing the inbox to shape their lives. Most successful CEOs meet regularly with faculty and staff organizations. These meetings allow people to express their frustrations and provide the opportunity to address problems early. I believe that communication and visibility are also important in reducing instances of incivility toward the leader, because it is easier to attack someone who is not known than someone who is familiar and seems reasonable, even if not all his or her decisions are to one's liking.

In addition, there are some refreshing examples of faculty, board, and administrative leaders that stating specific expectations for professional behavior. As an example, in November 2002, the Academic Senate at Mira Costa College in San Diego County published a pamphlet, *Collegiality, the Academic Senate, and Its Code of Ethics.* The code lists as responsibilities the expectation to model ethical behavior for students and colleagues; to treat colleagues and students with fairness and respect and without prejudice; to nurture a climate of mutual trust and support through honesty, open communication, and respect for academic freedom and the right to disagree; to protect students under college authority from conditions harmful to their health and safety; and to ensure that the rights of the group (class) do not suffer because of the inappropriate behavior of individual students.

The Association of Community College Trustees, through its publications, conferences, and board retreats, encourages boards to develop codes of ethics and helps board chairs to deal with inappropriate behavior on the part of individual board members. Trustee education is an important component of the mission of this organization. State trustee organizations also provide similar direction and services.

The American Association of Community Colleges has a model code of ethics for community college CEOs (see Appendix A). The code delineates values and responsibilities to constituents. AACC also supports the professional development of college leaders through the the AACC Presidents Academy, leader institutes, an annual convention, conferences, and publications.

Of course, codes of conduct do not always ensure good behavior. Ideally, the code should be endorsed by all campus constituencies. Although a code of conduct or code of ethics may not be all that is needed, it is clearly necessary to state what kind of behavior is expected. The code must be visibly displayed, and people need to be periodically reminded about the expectations that it sets. The topic of civility should be included as a part of orientation of new employees and new board members.

For example, support staff are essential to the operation of community colleges and are often the very first people contacted by students, prospective students, and community members, yet they are not always treated with respect by members of the campus community. Leaders must be sure to communicate the importance of these employees to the mission of the institution, and the codes of conduct must apply to how support staff members are treated. A class system for behavior toward employees has no place in the colleges of democracy.

All college leaders have a responsibility to create a campus climate in which people can teach, learn, and work free from threat or intimidation. The late Ernest Boyer made the following memorable recommendations for creating a strong campus community (Boyer, 1990; McDonald & Associates, 2002): The campus is an educationally purposeful community where faculty and students share academic goals and work together to strengthen teaching and learning.

- It is an open place where freedom of expression is protected and civility affirmed.
- It is a just community where sacredness of the person is honored and where diversity is aggressively pursued.
- It is a disciplined community where individuals accept their obligations to the group and where well-defined governance procedures guide behavior for the common good.
- It is a caring community where the well-being of each member is sensitively supported and where service to others is encouraged.
- It is a celebrative community where the heritage of the institution is remembered and where rituals affirming both tradition and change are widely shared.

Creating and maintaining a climate of trust and respect on our campuses is a responsibility all members of the campus community share. Community leaders, boards of trustees, administrators, faculty, staff, and students each can influence the environment on a campus by how we behave and how we respond to unacceptable behavior. The contributors to this book hope that the case studies and experiences shared and the advice provided make the case for the importance of this topic and encourage everyone involved in community colleges to help set a course for improved campus civility.

References

Boyer, E. (1990). *Campus life: In search of community.* San Francisco: The Carnegie Foundation for the Advancement of Teaching.

W. M. McDonald & Associates (2002). *Creating campus community: In search of Ernest Boyer's legacy.* San Francisco: Jossey-Bass.

CHAPTER ONE

Northern California Community Colleges in an Era of Dissent

Paul A. Elsner

In the late 1960s several issues—such as the controversy surrounding the war in Vietnam, the earlier free speech movement at the University of California—Berkeley (UC—Berkeley), and the insurgence of minorities pushing for civil rights and the sharing of power—caught many of us in college leadership roles off guard. No previous experience with these challenges had prepared us for this era. Most of us fell into situations we could hardly understand. We turned to our own resources, made mistakes, and learned some adaptive responses, but shock was the most characteristic response.

Suddenly, many college leaders found their campuses in the headlines. Firebombs, protest leading, and even campus takeovers were reported at Merritt College in the Peralta Community College District; standoffs with radical students at San Francisco State University and UC—Berkeley became the defining feature of higher education in the San Francisco Bay area; and many political movements extended out to Stanford University and to other parts of the state and country. The turmoil was further fueled by the assassinations of John F. Kennedy and Martin Luther King, Jr.

Many movements converged in the Berkeley area, most notably the Black power movement, epitomized by the Oakland Black Panthers confronting local police and even marching on the California Assembly in Sacramento. Students for a Democratic Society (SDS), headquartered in Boulder, Colorado, moved into the region, as did the Symbionese Liberation Army (SLA), the Black Panthers, La Raza (The Cause), the Hispanic GI Forum, and many other protest groups. This was a heady time—a time when we all had to come of age, with few guidelines and without the benefit of previous experience.

In 1967, I was distanced from most of these radical events. I was recruited by a newly formed board of directors to help establish the Colorado Community Colleges and Occupational Education System. At 33 years old, I was the youngest state director in the country. I was at the helm as local districts were dissolved as legal entities and condensed into an entirely state-funded community college system. The new district opened colleges in Denver, Colorado Springs, and other more rural areas of the state. We accomplished much in my short time there, with little disruption by the burgeoning movements in California; in fact, even though the SDS was headquartered in Boulder, we felt little of their effect at this time.

Peralta Community College District

In 1969, after just two years in Colorado, I had an opportunity to move to the Peralta Community College District, located in the heart of the Oakland–Berkeley area in California. The Peralta district consisted of four colleges: Merritt, Laney, Alameda, and Berkeley. I took the position of district director of educational services.

I was well aware of the revolutions occurring, especially in California, at this time; however, I was not fully prepared to find the most tumultuous of upheavals within the boundaries of the Peralta district. Although most disruptions were identified in association with the UC—Berkeley campus, many radical groups arrived daily to the Peralta district. For example, just the month before I arrived, a group of young student leaders, some loosely and some closely connected to the Oakland Black Panther Party, had locked the board of trustees in their boardroom at Merritt College. In an apparent attempt to intimidate the board, one of the student leaders placed a bullet before each of the five board members. The same minority students had demanded that more Blacks be placed in leadership roles and that the college be more sensitive to the increasing numbers of Black students enrolling.

In a short time, the staff at Merritt College had to become accustomed to having their campus overtaken by radical groups—some peaceful, some not. Although most takeovers served to assert students' Black power, occasionally Hispanic or White students participated, joining the spirit of revolution and seeking recognition of their power as well. Sit-ins were generally peaceful; protesting students simply sat for hours in order to be recognized. At other times, radical students acted on their threats of firebombs, campus takeovers, and the like. In one incident, reporters claimed that the portable buildings at Merritt College had been firebombed. Although this particular report proved to be untrue, college personnel warned the district that the old administration building—with its aging, dry, wood floors and paneling—was vulnerable to a fire assault by the radical students. We faced risks like this almost daily. Sometimes, the attackers had no specific group affiliation; even so, various groups usually claimed credit for aggressive acts. Some groups were not known to us at the time. Later, we learned that many organizations operated on and off the Peralta campuses: SDS, SLA, the Hispanic GI Forum, The Weathermen, and many others.

Relocating Merritt College

In the 1960s, a $47 million bond was passed for the Peralta Community College District—at the time, the largest bond in the country. This bond was intended to facilitate the building of four new campuses. Two of those campuses— Alameda and Berkeley—would be built where none had previously existed, which would accommodate the growing population of students coming of age. Laney and Merritt were old and in need of updated facilities. Although the Berkeley campus was never built, the other three campuses were under construction around the time of my arrival.

At this time, much tension resulted from the relocation of the existing Merritt Community College to a more well-to-do neighborhood. At its original location on Grove Street the college served poor, Black students predominantly, along with some White students from Berkeley. The new location could potentially prevent the local population from taking advantage of the community college experience. Those opposed to the move rallied to keep the campus at its original location, but they were unsuccessful. In the end, the new campus was built at the new site, albeit with protest. Community members, radical students, and even some faculty rallied to stop movement of equipment from the old site to the new. To avoid inciting any violent episodes, the district worked through the middle of several nights to extricate and relocate the equipment under the protection of security guards and police escorts.

The Community Control Movement

At about the same time, the community around the old campus rallied to create a "community control" movement. The concept of community control of schools grew out of Chicago and New York, where minorities served by larger city school districts felt short-changed by the inferior quality of their schools. Community control encouraged greater self-determination at the local level for basic literacy, as well as the appointment of more minorities to local advisory or control boards, and higher-quality standards for their school systems. This movement became a rallying cry in Oakland, just as in other U.S. cities, sparked by those in society who were seeking more equity in education.

During this time, Peralta's chancellor, John Dunn, was often called to forums throughout the state to interpret the radical uprisings on the Peralta and

San Francisco State campuses; this was often done with San Francisco State's president, S. I. Hayakawa, who became a powerful and visible force in battling student radicals. Because the Peralta Community College District, UC—Berkeley, and San Francisco State were geographically close, many of the same radical groups aappeared on all the campuses, seemingly moving from one to another. Conservative politicians from Orange County and other parts of California would hold press conferences in places like Walnut Creek and Marin County, decrying the disrespect and total breakdown of authority in places like Peralta, Berkeley, and San Francisco State. It amused Peralta staff members to think that the politicians probably avoided coming into Alameda County or the Berkeley–Oakland area because it was too unsafe; they always voiced their outrage from the safety of their more sheltered world.

About a year after my arrival, Chancellor Dunn took a sabbatical leave. The vice chancellor for business affairs became the interim chancellor. I moved up to a de facto vice chancellor role, for which one of my first assignments was to write a position paper on community control on behalf of the board and interim chancellor. This paper was intended to provide a format for community control, the momentum for which was coming from the community.

I presented the paper at a board meeting of the Peralta Community College District. Unexpectedly, more than 800 people attended. Among the crowd was a gifted Black orator and community organizer, who rallied the audience by speaking in favor of community control. The audience was awed by this skilled speaker; at crescendos, the audience stomped its feet on the all-wooden floors of the auditorium. The noise in the auditorium was deafening. The crowd cheered for the speaker and vocally implored the board to pass a community control resolution.

The meeting was held at the Oakland Public Schools auditorium, with the Oakland police attack-and-assault squads poised outside at the perimeter because of limited standing and seating space. The police were taking no chances, as this building was a site of well-known violence in Oakland. Earlier that year, Oakland Superintendent of Schools Marcus Foster had been gunned down and killed on the same site.

The tension, the air of danger, and the incendiary potential of this meeting could have easily escalated. At one point, a board member suggested that the community control action item be deferred to a subsequent meeting, prompting the audience to burst into a thunderous uproar. After sitting through three hours of speakers making the case for community control, the audience demanded an immediate roll call vote on the passage or rejection of the community control board item. Essentially, it created a secondary board that would advise on the direction of the local college from neighborhood interests.

The community control action concept passed 4 to 1. The results of the vote shot through the Oakland and Berkeley communities. To some, it was seen as an abrogation of the board's authority; to others, it was seen as a mandate for local self-determination in a college area affected by racial tensions. Earlier developments at Peralta had set a pattern for this upheaval: When the new Merritt College campus was to open, the old campus was to close. In addition, a third campus was opening at Alameda, an island community off Oakland's east bay.

One of my tasks upon arriving at Peralta was to move 165 faculty members from the old Merritt facility. Many faculty members were already disturbed about the radicalization of old Merritt College. Many wanted to move to Alameda's new college, because it was viewed as a refuge for the shell-shocked staff that had suffered through violent overthrows and virtual anarchy at Merritt. For each transfer, I had to negotiate acceptance by the new president of Alameda, Earnest Berg. We were concerned that some faculty had race-related motivations for seeking a transfer to Alameda. We agreed, with Dunn's blessing, that a balanced staff—with respect to race as well as attitude—was the only way we could achieve future peace in Peralta.

Once we had coordinated 140 successful transfers with all parties signed off, reaching the 165 goal became very difficult. Tension and anger arose. Faculty were concerned about leaving Merritt but were faced with the possibility of not being able to transfer to another campus. Threatening phone calls to me became persistent. Some came from angered minorities, who accused me of arranging a passage for racially biased faculty to Alameda. Nonminority faculty accused me of stacking a desirable mix of ethnic and racial groups to keep specific nonminority faculty out of contention for transfer. I received threats to my family and to my life; I was told that I would be run off and that my job would be lost. When we reached 161 transfers, the threats intensified. I asked Chancellor Dunn, before he took his leave, if we could stop at 160, hoping the remaining transfers would solve themselves. He agreed, and tension subsided.

Campuses split from each other, trust weakened, and recriminations of all kinds were directed toward and received by faculty and administrators alike; the tension and pressure from the outside finally infiltrated a large part of the community college system. Some faculty members aligned themselves with coalitions to throw out the board based on the board's perceived capitulation to the militancy of the Oakland auditorium crowds. Such actions were seen to have forced the passing of the community control resolution.

In all, it was a time when citizens were thrown into fear, doubt, and concern for the stability of the society. Following the turmoil of the Berkeley free speech movements over several months, the Black Panthers were having shootouts with the Oakland police. Students from UC—Berkeley, San Francisco State, San Jose State, and Stanford were constantly in revolt over issues of free speech and the Vietnam War. Boards, such as Peralta's, were seen as weakened by the radicalism.

Attempt to Regain Order

A handful of faculty leaders and staff ran a "law and order" board, which the press called the Peralta Five. Essentially, the board's main objective was to achieve order. At the time, I was waiting for implementation procedures for the aforementioned community control mandate. I thought it was an important and timely piece of work, modernist in tone as well as socially constructive and innovative. Unfortunately, upon Dunn's return from sabbatical, the project was jettisoned. At about the same time, Dunn began his transition to the chancellorship of a nearby district on the peninsula of the San Francisco bay area. He recommended that I be appointed as permanent vice chancellor, a position that I later assumed.

Through all the turmoil, I learned that the power of a few individuals can reshape the direction of a whole district. This was brought home in the election of the Peralta Five—although to be accurate, only four on the slate were elected. A fifth person was running on his own grievance: He had not been hired as a full-time instructor. Having been dropped as a continuous part-time employee, he initiated a lawsuit to regain his position but lost. After appealing to a higher court, he won his job back, as well as a seat on the board.

I took away from Peralta a growing understanding of why dissent occurs. Scarcely any minorities held either teaching or leadership positions—one source of dissent that made some radicalism politically necessary. At the same time, a number of the faculty and staff were "in flight" from the civil unrest they experienced at the old Merritt campus, which had become a predominantly Black college whose student leadership consisted of several radical framers and architects of the Black liberation movement. Many faculty and staff were simply not prepared for or easily disposed to such rapid political and demographic shifts.

The larger community of Oakland, as well as all of California and the nation, became riveted to the events at Peralta and in Berkeley. At one time, the

Black Panthers, fully armed, managed to walk into the chambers of the California legislative assembly in Sacramento before they were finally detained. Skirmishes between them and the Oakland police were frequently reported in the media. Many national figures in the Black liberation movement were regular students at Merritt College and the other Peralta Community College District campuses. Although they had a reputation as radicals, the Black Panthers also offered ideas for impressive social programs such as nutritious food and milk for infants and children and day care centers—programs Peralta later adopted for all of its campuses.

The Hispanic Presence

Hispanic groups were also forming in California. La Raza was present on several California campuses. Groups like the Hispanic GI Forum and Chicano movements in Colorado and Texas began to expand to California. Hard-core groups like the loosely connected Soledad Brothers began in prisons and became better known after the media covered their activities.

Chancellor Dunn once asked me to mediate a case involving a Skill Center employee and member of the GI Forum who had thrown a lethal welding rod at a Black teacher, just missing him and nicking his ear. The Skill Center was in near riot; had both parties not disappeared immediately, the Skill Center would have probably been burned down. In another incident, an employee was shot to death through the window of his bedroom as a result of a sales territory dispute involving bakery sales. As vice chancellor for academic and student affairs, I was often called on to listen to students' concerns and demands. Sometimes listening was a better response than reacting. Sometimes I was afraid, but I trained myself to look as though I was not.

I later became president of a nontraditional college in Berkeley called the Peralta College of Non-Traditional Study (PCNS). Now called Vista College, PCNS was actually a storefront college that had three presidents before I became CEO. The college was located near downtown Berkeley, not far off Telegraph Avenue and near People's Park, the political epicenter of upheaval in Berkeley in the late 1970s. People's Park was a neighborhood icon. The area sought self-determination by promoting its own lifestyle and the freedom to congregate, particularly in public spaces for celebration, rallies, food bazaars, and political organization. Many traditional Berkeley residents saw the park as an eyesore—noisy, raucous, and generally not conducive to maintaining a quiet neighborhood. Planning officials and municipal interests tried to dissolve the park, but advocates of the park resisted the idea of its use being dictated by the City of Berkeley. The presidency in Berkeley was considered by most everyone in the know at Peralta as the Coffin Corner, as many recent presidents had either been fired or had quit their position out of frustration. At about this time, the five-college Maricopa system in Phoenix called for the national recruitment of a chancellor. I decided to apply.

Maricopa Community College District

Before arriving at Maricopa, I received communications from a group of faculty who had been frustrated in their attempt to put forward a nontraditional college. Their aim was to have a broader outreach and to provide a more on-demand model for providing services to senior citizens, the poor, and the disadvantaged—many of whom were minorities in the community. Because of my experience with PCNS, an outreach-oriented nontraditional college, this small group seemed to welcome my arrival. It became evident, however, that any prospects this small group had to create a nontraditional college were to be indefinitely postponed. I should have read the warnings better. At that time, the Maricopa community colleges had been under siege because of disruptions among the students at Scottsdale Community College and among its board, which had seated two students as board members.

My predecessor had been removed in a coup led by what was, in my opinion, the radical portion of the board. It was hard to decipher exactly what had been transpiring before my arrival; as a new CEO, I learned that not many people were willing to share information for my benefit. Luckily, I had a few occasions to associate with my predecessor. Although this man may have had enormous justification for showing anger and could have discredited the board for which I now worked, he was the most ethically centered professional I had ever met. Even when I expressed frustration, he never said a negative word about the district, the players, or the board members who allegedly ousted him with the help of several faculty members.

As chancellor, I recommended to the board that we construct a nontraditional college, whose major purpose was to enhance outreach types of programs. It was intended to create more methods of delivering instruction, such as television courses, radio courses, or even correspondence courses. The college was able to model its programs on successful outreach programs at several of its existing traditional colleges. The Maricopa board approved the formation of Rio Salado College; the district then went into major political uproar.

Glendale Community College, part of the Maricopa system, held rallies against Rio Salado College, although the two student board representatives encouraged its formation. Votes of censure followed. Protestors created a tombstone—quite well crafted—with an inscription that implied that quality education had died upon my arrival. "Here lies quality education" continued to be the rallying metaphor in attacks against the newly formed nontraditional Rio Salado College. The attacks challenged the quality of the college's television courses, such as an American history course that had been leased from the Dallas County Community College District, and other attacks targeted philosophy offerings. One community-based course in religious studies sparked much controversy aimed at its coordinator and the credentials of the religious studies instructor.

Nontraditional colleges had emerged around the country, and their formation sometimes caused bitter debate in the national higher education community. Moreover, having come directly from a presidency of one such college apparently stigmatized me as a "nontraditional," making me a scapegoat for the angst, fear, and animosities that characterized the protest. Rumors were spreading that I, as well as the new vice chancellors, would be fired. Some faculty members were researching my background and those of the staff I had brought on board. After being subjected to many transgressions and violations of professionalism, I decided that some jobs are not worth having under the wrong conditions. So, to the shock of the board, the internal community, and to some of the outside community, I resigned a year and a half into my tenure. At the board's request, I agreed to attend a retreat session with the broader internal community for the purposes of adopting a code of ethics and conduct. I did not set this as a condition for returning, although I did return eventually. At the time I just thought that such deliberation might help the board and the district.

To this day, the board's code still exists. It has been seriously violated on some occasions. I do not advocate resigning and then returning. After I agreed to return, I enjoyed at least 15 years of principled conduct by the board, but the ethics code did not always hold. The board did not sanction the behavior of the other board members when such sanctions were needed. A code works only when the total trust of its members causes them to respect it. Chancellors should leave in the face of the unprincipled behavior I describe. They really should not return even in the best of concessions or conditions.

■ ■ ■

I worked with excellent board members at Peralta and at Maricopa to whom I am much indebted. I admired the liberal Peralta board and came to respect the Peralta law and order board. I worked well with board members of whom I was not necessarily fond; I did not choose board members—voters did. Board members who were opposed to me gave me lessons I needed to learn about myself. Such lessons included a greater need for patience and the realization that one needs to make things work with the people with whom one works. Together, we did that well.

CHAPTER TWO

Lessons in Leadership When Tradition and Change Collide

Martha Gandert Romero

Increasingly, community colleges struggle to maintain a culture in which civility and conflict can coexist and the energy generated by conflict can be redirected to produce creative and innovative solutions to problems. Our colleges need to be models for our society by responding to differences of ideology and practice between leaders and their constituents in nonviolent and nonhostile ways. Unfortunately, within our colleges we often respond to disagreement aggressively and with a general lack of civility.

My goal in this chapter is to record, as accurately as I am able, a set of events that severely disrupted the college and community in which I served as CEO. Although I realize my memory will be somewhat selective, I have tried to be objective in stating the facts of the situation and drawing conclusions about responding to conflict from which I and other community college CEOs can learn. As one gains experience, the perspectives of any action can take on different meanings; therefore, the conclusions I draw today may be colored by my life experiences and may represent perspectives as seen through my current experiential lens.

This story is about conflict between a community and its community college. Conflict is seldom rational as it unfolds, but in retrospect, four themes emerged over a three-year period that I feel are instructive for community colleges everywhere. First, in hiring new leadership, a college may affirm that change is needed at the same time it resists change in favor of tradition and the status quo. Second, the community college boardroom can become the arena for conflicts between values of higher education and values of the community. Third, when there is a threat to the values of higher education from outside the college, those in leadership positions—which in the best case includes the CEO, the board, and the faculty—all have a stake in defending those values. Finally, change in a college may be strengthened if the college successfully defends its core values in an open conflict.

Community colleges by name and design have roots in their communities. When change comes through a new CEO, the change will reverberate throughout the entire community—the board, the faculty and staff, local political organizations, service clubs, minority groups, etc. This is especially true when the previous administration has been in place for 23 years as it had when this college hired a new CEO in 1992. In the best case, the various community groups will affirm the new form of the organization that results from change. However, the process of change may reveal exactly where those long and deep community roots attach and exactly where the values of the college and the values of the community conflict.

In small communities, change comes slowly or not at all. People tend to believe that jobs are for life. The desirability of a position is determined by its stability. Thus, the criterion of greatest interest to community members when a new CEO is appointed is whether the candidate is making a lifetime commitment to the position. So, too, people in other levels of administration, or faculty or staff for that matter, typically believe they will progress in their careers exclusively inside the college. The leadership pool and the opportunities for developing leadership skills tend to be small in colleges of this size. The longtime leadership of a faculty may lack the energy or will to invest in change efforts.

In the district where I came to serve as CEO in 1992, the community and the campus were initially vocal about their approval and excitement that a change of leadership was occurring. In the absence of recent experience with major change, however, many people did not anticipate that old assumptions, patterns of behavior, and entrenched procedures would be subject to great change. In the community, suspicions about how the college functioned—which had built up over years—continued to plague the college after I arrived. Some staff members whose success had resulted from maneuvering in the old system were unprepared to change old behaviors and learn new skills. Those who benefited from being a part of the previous mode of operation were threatened by their perceived decrease in status.

Many employees expressed appreciation that I took a participatory rather than autocratic role as CEO of the college and that I intended to open the process of information sharing rather than withhold information in a way that would confer status on a selected few. I upgraded the already established CEO's council—composed of the traditional senior vice presidents, the academic senate representative, the classified senate representative (who in this case was also the classified union representative), and a representative of the classified managers group—to a larger cabinet.

New members of the cabinet included the personnel director, the public information officer, and the development officer, all of whom were reassigned to report directly to me. These changes in structure challenged many old ways of doing business at the college. Some former senior administrators were reluctant to hold open discussions in the cabinet and were silent at meetings; afterward, however, they conducted long discussions by memorandum or spoke among themselves about decisions being influenced by people in the organization without their level of education or position status. Other cabinet members challenged the authority of council members to participate in problem-solving discussions that might go against their constituent group's tradition. Could a union representative, for example, really participate in an open discussion about staffing or budgeting? The challenge did not come from the union representative but from a member of the senior administrative team. To me these examples served as evidence of the need for training and, in some cases, staffing changes in order to operate successfully under a new set of values.

In addition, the perceived new freedom to raise issues and advance agendas caused discussion of long-suppressed conflicts to surface. The college faculty, who had not unionized (unions are the norm rather than the exception in this state), perhaps because they feared the reaction of the former CEO, began discussions of forming a union almost immediately after I came. For the next five years, faculty discussed forming a union, and after two elections they were successful. My administration took the position that if the faculty chose to unionize, the administration would support their efforts, recognizing that the college would lose some problem-solving flexibility.

Although many people supported the idea of a faculty union on principle, only faculty who had not previously held faculty leadership roles became the leaders, and as with all unseasoned leaders, they made mistakes, sometimes because of assumptions based on previously held values. For example, the new leaders understood their roles only as messengers, not as representatives able to participate in making decisions.

Like all community colleges in this state, the college struggled with the legislative mandate for shared governance. Among the values drawn into question by shared governance were beliefs about the role of the college CEO. Who had ultimate authority to make decisions? Did the faculty report directly to the trustees and not the CEO in the areas listed in the legislation? More than once the cabinet collectively reflected on "Whose job is on the line for this decision?" New faculty leaders often refused to participate in decisions, claiming they were only message carriers with no authority to act without consulting the entire faculty for a vote. The statewide academic senate added to the confusion as it struggled to make sense of the role of faculty in each of the 11 legislatively mandated governance areas. The tug-of-war was over power, not responsibility. No one spoke much of individual or even functional responsibility. One could say the value of individual responsibility was understood only as placing blame and identifying the corresponding actions of reprisal. Functional responsibility seemed to be applied only to me as the college CEO, and I was challenged on nearly every decision I made.

Within the first month after my arrival, the board and I agreed to consider change in several vice presidential appointments. I asked the board for one year to work with existing staff and promised a recommendation at the end of the year. The board members, in turn, agreed to support my recommendation when it came to them. At the end of my first year, I recommended reassignment of two of the three vice presidents to faculty positions. For the first, there was total agreement by the board and the college community; with the second, there were differences of opinion both on the board and within the college community.

When the second vice president was reassigned, a tenured faculty member—who had been reprimanded for displaying inappropriate behavior toward students—decided to take his issues to the press and to combine his campaign against the administration with that of the second vice president. He claimed a violation of his academic freedom. Meanwhile, unrelated problematic behavior of the controller (who also functioned as chief accountant) created a situation that required the board and CEO to call for his immediate release.

The faculty and staff had responded neutrally to the reorganization of the committees and changes in business procedures, but the personnel decisions created a furor. These four critical personnel changes, although unrelated to one another, were collectively the impetus for what became a concerted effort to unseat me and the board of trustees. I believe the actions to reassign two vice presidents to faculty positions (a guarantee by state policy to administrators hired before 1990) probably would not have created a problem had they not been accompanied by the faculty personnel action and by the action to release the controller and chief accountant, an at-will employee.

The combination of these four actions and the resulting uncertainty in what changes would occur next highlighted the dysfunctional nature of the system. According to chaos literature, disequilibria is essential for change and growth to occur (Wheatley, 1992, p. 78); yet, people do not set out to create instability in a system. In our case, once set in motion, the combined force of these changes energized the community to test the resolve of the new CEO, the board, and the college itself over a 20-month period.

The Boardroom as Arena for a Clash of Values

The boardroom as an arena for the clash between community and college values is illustrated in the case of the dismissed controller introduced earlier. I learned of the controller's misconduct when the personnel director sent two employees to report that the controller had just told them, "I've got them now." "Them" referred to me and to the controller's immediate supervisor, the vice president for administrative services. The controller indicated that the books would show that the district reserves were spent and the college "was broke." The staff members said they had asked the controller whether he had informed his supervisor or the CEO, to which the controller replied: "No, they are paid the big bucks to figure that out, but I've taken actions to inform the public." Later on the same day, the front page of the local newspaper carried the story that the district had spent its reserves and was in serious financial trouble.

The vice president and I immediately put the controller on a paid leave of absence. Our primary concern was whether the books had been kept in such a way as to mask real overspending. If the controller continued in his role, we believed we would not be able to conduct a definitive analysis.

In proceeding with the personnel matter, we called upon the advice of the district's attorney. We called in our audit firm and requested a thorough audit of the district's books. We also requested a loaned staff person from the state chancellor's office who was knowledgeable about state regulation and financial reporting to help determine the extent of our problems. The district eventually learned through the special audit that in order to make it appear that the district had spent its reserves, a number of entries for long-term obligations had been posted against the existing budget. The audit revealed that the district was fiscally healthy and stable.

Next, we had to consider the removal of the controller. Legal counsel proposed two optional personnel actions. The first was to use a recent law, which held that any employee not represented by a bargaining unit or serving under contract served at the pleasure of the board (i.e., "at will") and could be released by the board without cause. The second was to develop a case and fire the employee for cause. Building a case against the employee would take weeks and perhaps months, during which time the disgruntled controller could conceivably cause irreparable damage while the district continued to incur salary costs. The district chose the first option and released the controller as an at-will employee. The board meeting at which this action took place was a particularly sensitive one because the attorney and I could not describe the extent of the employee's wrongdoing without moving into a discussion of cause. The board decided to trust the attorney and me and supported our recommendation. There was one dissenting voice.

At the next board meeting, the former controller brought the congregation of his fundamentalist church community to the meeting. Also present were a number of constitutionalists reputedly affiliated with the "unorganized militia of the county." Circumstances conspired to make an uncomfortable meeting unbearable. Because the main campus administrative building was under renovation and a number of open trenches surrounded the building where board meetings were usually held, the meeting was scheduled at the satellite campus in one of the available classrooms. Previously scheduled final exams prevented our using a larger facility on the main campus. (A strongly held value of the instructional unit is to provide optimal testing conditions for students. The instructor and academic vice president strongly recommended not moving students for a timed final exam.) Unfortunately, the room scheduled for the board meeting was small and did not accommodate the number of people who showed up to address the board. In addition, rain was falling hard on the evening of the meeting. Although all participants were sheltered in another classroom and everyone who wanted to address the board had the opportunity to do so, the group that had mobilized in support of the former controller felt insulted and mistreated.

The combination of staff changes, discontented citizens, the rain, and the perceived change in the status quo galvanized that night an effort to recall all but the one board member who had voted against the immediate release of the controller. Before it was over, the instigators of the recall, aided by a few staff members, would be responsible for two costly elections: one special election and one heavily contested regular election with serious challenges to the board members and the CEO. Election results are described in the next section.

During the next two years, church members and constitutionalists attended every board meeting. Sometimes they read scripture passages during the public input. Other times, they read constitutionalist material concerning how they were not bound by the laws of the state but only by the U.S.

Constitution. One of their constituency, a cowboy poet on whose property the militia reputedly held its training, openly berated me, a Hispanic female CEO. The conflict became a proxy for community-held values against race, gender roles, and representative democracy.

Several months after the controller was released, the chair of the board resigned because he accepted the superintendency of the largest high school district in the county and believed it would be a conflict of interest for him to continue on the board. The board exercised its option to appoint a replacement for the vacancy as provided by state law. The board accepted applications from interested people who could represent the geographic area served by the previous board member. After review of the three applications received, the board appointed an individual to serve until the next election. The group of dissidents immediately launched an attack on the board's appointment. Although they publicly stated they had nothing against the appointed member, this was one board action they could attack easily. They acquired the necessary signatures to force a special election. Elections are conducted at district expense. The cost is always significant, although the exact cost varies depending on whether other items sponsored by other organizations are on the ballot. In this case, the cost was borne entirely by the district because no other items were on the ballot. Ironically, the detractors regularly accused the board of spending district funds frivolously. They were especially vocal about the funds used to bring a Bay area attorney to work with the district.

The special election was held in August 1995 to decide between the appointed board member, one other candidate who had applied for the position, and a third candidate who by his own admission was enlisted by the opposition. This third candidate's main qualification was that he lived in the isolated geographic area in which the candidates must reside. After the election, in a moment of rare candor, he revealed that the people who had encouraged him to run had told him he would have to attend only one meeting a month and "they would do all the rest." He was elected by 18 votes. The constitutionalist members found a judge friendly to their cause to immediately swear him in (successful board candidates are usually sworn in by the clerk of the board at the first meeting). A picture of the swearing in was in the newspaper the day after the election.

At the first meeting, the chair of the Foundation Board, acting not as a foundation member but as a private citizen, challenged the legality of the new member's service on the board. He asked the board to investigate evidence that the new board member was a convicted felon and asked whether a felon could serve on the board. The board chair indicated that he would refer the matter to counsel. In the interim, the board member was fully installed and accepted as a board member. (We subsequently learned that in this state a felon can serve on a publicly elected board, as long as he or she is no longer on probation.)

Although the new board member often called for a roll call vote, he regularly abstained from voting. At the first meeting he tried to tape record the closed session of the board using a tape recorder placed in his open briefcase, but board members were vigilant and quickly stopped that action. The newly elected board member served for six months and then resigned. Upon resigning, he sued the district for stress. He also filed suit for defamation against the man who asked the board to look into his record. The courts denied both claims. After his resignation, the board reappointed the unseated member because he was the candidate who had received the second-largest number of votes.

The dissident group continued for a year to collect enough signatures to hold a recall election against the board members who had voted to release the controller. The board member who did not vote with the others later told the board that she had continued to meet with the dissident group to try to understand their perspective. When she eventually failed to provide them information or carry their agenda to the board, she, too, became subjected to anonymous harassment. She then better understood why board members cannot act as individuals but only as members who make up one entity, the board.

Three members were up for reelection within several months (1995) and so were legally exempt from recall. One church member and one constitutionalist "relocated" to areas represented by these board members and ran against them. The district filed a complaint with the State Election Board because these candidates were not residents of the areas they were seeking to represent. The address the constitutionalist listed as his new home was inhabited by a couple who told the local newspaper that the candidate sometimes stayed with them but did not live there. The election board said they had so many complaints, they would investigate at a later time when their caseload lessened, but in the meantime the candidates could continue to run as filed. To date, no response has been received from the compliance agency.

Up to this point, the college faculty and staff appeared to be taking a wait-and-see attitude; after the special election in 1995, however, they came to life when the recall elections were announced in 1996. It became clear to them that it was possible for the college board to be dominated by the religious right and the militia if they continued to be inactive. Leaders in the community who had taken a hands-off approach to the issues mobilized to respond. The three sitting board members were reelected with decisive majorities. At that point, only the two remaining board members were subject to face recall in the second special election held in February 1996, again at the expense of the district. Once again the internal and external communities rallied, and the sitting board members were returned to office.

With the defeats in the election, the dissident group stopped coming to the board meetings and addressing the board. One church member returned several meetings later to ask the board's forgiveness and to share with them that in his opinion the group had lost interest. The community that initially rallied around the dissidents ultimately found their tactics and position extreme and distasteful and stood up for the college and its duly appointed administration. The lawsuits filed by the former controller were settled out of court upon the recommendation of the district's insurance company some five years after the recall election. The issue raised in the newspapers was that settling a case must signal that the college and its administrators were guilty. A local attorney who had defended the controller early in the fray was quoted to that effect. The fact that insurance companies recommend settling before a trial because they can thereby limit their financial liability against expensive court trials is little known or understood in these circles. It is one of the anomalies of the U.S. justice system that is truly difficult to live with as a college CEO and board member. The financial prudence of such action, however, is unassailable when one understands how the system works.

Defending the Values of Higher Education

As a microcosm of a democratic society, a community college requires that each constituency take seriously its responsibility to affirm the values of the college as an embodiment of a civil society. The CEO, the board, and the faculty have a stake in defending the values of higher education from external threats. All have a stake in creating an environment in which people can express differences without attempting to destroy those whose views they oppose. At the same time, each key constituency within the college shares a set of common values. At times of great unrest, a few discontented staff members can marshal support of community opposition groups and use this influence to drive personal agendas that are not congruent with those of higher education. The board and CEO will be on public display as citizens try to understand the issues and decide who is right.

In the situation I have described, citizens—including staff people, both those who supported and those who opposed the board and administration—attended every board meeting and carefully scrutinized the board's behavior. What did we put on closed session agendas? Were we violating the open meeting law? Could they place items on the board's agenda? How?

A revision in the Open Meeting law prevented the board from responding or holding impromptu discussions on issues raised by anyone at a board meeting unless the item had been formally placed on the agenda at least one week ahead of the meeting. This protected the board during this time and raised the conflict level between board members and citizens who came with long lists of questions and counterpoints in an effort to fuel the controversy at hand. The statute allows the board to respond to factual questions or seek clarification of statements or questions if they do not understand, but it does not allow the board to engage in discussion. For example, one open session question was "What does the board think of having a CEO who cares so little for students that she suspended a student who used a college credit card to call her family in a foreign country?" The board responded with "The board has a policy for the appropriate use of college credit cards and a policy to evaluate the CEO." The board would have no further discussion. This policy is an important tool for maintaining control of the agenda for the board and for citizens who might want to be present for a particular discussion.

The dissidents made frequent requests for records, especially on fiscal reporting procedures that only insiders would know by name. On-campus individuals copied records to supply to the outside group, sometimes officially, sometimes subversively. At a local elementary school, the husband of one college employee was seen making copies of internal college documents. On another occasion, flyers describing "How to take over the schools" mysteriously appeared in the copying machines across the campus. The information in the flyers appeared to accurately catalog what was occurring on the campus.

People on campus who were perceived as supporting the board and administration were openly challenged, and their behaviors and records were scrutinized for impropriety or mistakes. The state chancellor's office, the congressional offices, and a number of state regulatory agencies received and investigated complaints filed by the former controller. All of these actions took inordinate amounts of time, tied up staff energy, and cast a cloud of suspicion on the district board and administration. In some instances, minor adjustments were made as a result of staff reporting mistakes, but no impropriety was discovered. These behaviors all appeared to be designed to cause havoc, consume staff time, and bring the college to a standstill. One resulting consequence was that there was less staff time and energy available to bring about needed change.

What is clear to me in retrospect is that the coalition to oppose change shared religious, political, ideological, gender, and to a lesser extent, racial values, which differed from those of the college leadership. Ultimately, the campus and external communities realized the resistance movement represented much more than disagreement with the decision to release or reassign a few employees. The clash of values threatened the life of the institution of higher education and our democratic way of life. A special-interest group was attempting to seize control of the public college board. To its credit, this board had undertaken extensive training, had established a code of ethics for its own behavior, and had set policy guidelines to evaluate its own performance annually about the same time that it evaluated the college CEO.

Board chairs are under extraordinary pressure in such environments, and managing meetings effectively within the law becomes difficult. Our board chairs were skilled, but the entire board agreed to remain vigilant to points of order, control, and decorum throughout this challenging period. As elected officials, they were aware of the spotlight that was on them. They understood the difference between the information they could provide their constituents and confidential information about college business that they could not share with the public. They invested personal time away from their other responsibilities informing the community and presenting their case as allowed by law.

With the failure of the recall, the climate on campus calmed, and the values of higher education were reaffirmed. The long-lasting effects of such a challenge continued to be felt, however, and the board and I sought ways to establish a center from which to continue to support the values and changes we had caused to happen. Board members and staff set an example of higher education leadership in trying times. President George Norlin articulated a standard of such leadership well during the challenge to the University of Colorado by the Ku Klux Klan in 1925: He challenged his university "to be courageous in the midst of panic, to cherish liberty in the midst of its excesses, to go forward even when progress is in disrepute" (Knox, 1997).

Lessons Learned

CEOs learn while everyone watches, and everyone is quick to critique their actions. Even inexperienced or unsophisticated media professionals may believe that it is their right to report every nuance that others observe. In my situation, a fundamentalist church community and the rumored unorganized militia members joined hands to oppose my actions as college CEO and as the highest-paid public employee (and female and Hispanic) in the county. Before it was over, entire communities took positions for or against my decisions and added to the debate whatever longstanding issue they had left over from other times.

As I reflect on this time now, with some geographic and emotional distance, I continue to learn. With each effort to tell the story and reflect on its meaning, I understand the loneliness of my position at that time. It strengthens my belief that CEOs have an ongoing responsibility to sort and sift and find new meaning in order to prepare leaders who will encounter situations that will test their values and practices in novel and unexpected situations. It also is apparent to me that CEOs need access to coaches who are outside the environment who can provide objective support and perspective.

Not only is a CEO's learning public, but a CEO's responses while under attack are public. The leader cannot demonstrate vulnerability, because if the opposing forces are strong enough, any sign of weakness in the CEO jeopardizes the college. After the board recall had failed and I was no longer under attack, I learned that staff were taking their cues from my behavior about how they should behave.

Several support staff—whose jobs were to videotape the board meetings—told me that on several occasions they were angry and thought about responding physically but were always restrained by the fact that I remained cool. One said, "You did not take them on, but you also did not look beaten by them." I felt increasing pressure to model reasonable behavior even as the tenor of the personal attacks against me grew stronger and became more verbal.

Occasionally, someone would ask if I felt physically endangered, and sometimes I did. Regardless of how I felt, I responded by minimizing my perceived sense of danger. I knew by the relief and demeanor of those who asked that my response was what they were seeking as reassurance. During such times, a CEO is the model that will keep others productive or will cause the organization's effectiveness to deteriorate.

Many of the dissenters' strategies were aimed at trying to make me respond as an offender. Sometimes the meanings assigned to my actions as sanctions against those criticizing me were somewhat comical. For example, the dissenters derided the board for creating a situation wherein tax dollars were spent in litigation. They had a hand in the litigation, of course, but the implication was that if I were not the CEO, the litigation would be unnecessary.

In addition to the challenge of leadership, I felt my behavior was modeling behavior for our female professionals and students about appropriate or inappropriate responses to abusive situations. Many were the evenings when I came home to read the literature on abuse and appropriate coping behavior. The literature on abuse conflicts with the literature on leadership. The prevailing advice for abuse is, "Get out of the situation." The literature on leadership provides an escape hatch: "Leave when you can no longer be effective"; but it describes as exemplary those leaders who remain strong and constant in the face of crisis. After the crisis was over, several faculty members told me they had learned about persevering and facing difficult situations and indicated that the college was stronger as a result of my tenacity.

The dissident group, as well as the former controller and faculty member, had been vocal about the role of women. I was vulnerable to their history of complaints about women taking men's jobs or otherwise behaving in ways that challenged male supremacy. What I did, I knew, would have far-reaching effects for other women who have positions of leadership in our country. In *Leadership Without Easy Answers*, Heifetz (1996) indicated that issues are often used as proxies for conflicts that threaten a way of life. For me, the issues were not only gender related but racial as well. This was one instance in which being accustomed to dealing with issues of gender and race in other school and career situations served me well.

Heifetz said that personalizing a problem as in "if we had the right leader" is a way to regulate the disequilibria being brought to a cultural system. To respond personally gives the strategy credence and strength and perpetuates the dynamics. Separating oneself from one's role is a critical leadership skill. To survive such a situation, a CEO must be able to separate herself from her role. Furthermore, one must distinguish between taking personal responsibility and internalizing a conflict as personal. This is a dispassionate and reasoned statement. To live that distinction is another matter entirely.

Only a well-functioning board can survive this kind of challenge. The board and I agreed from the beginning to hold four retreats a year. We had an established code of ethics and held annual board evaluation sessions. At that time, if one board member had an issue with the behavior of any other board member, he or she called for a special board evaluation session and aired the concern. The board was particularly diligent during board meetings to ensure that all members operated within the law, and try as it might, the dissident group was unable to fault the board for its behavior.

The two board chairs who served during this time were particularly adept at ensuring that the dissident group members were allowed to make their presentations without giving away control of the board meeting. The board and I tried to take the high road and not react to the provocations that were leveled at us. On one occasion an abusive, dissonant group member interrupted me to say to our board chair: "Bill, be the man that you are and tell her to shut up." The board chair simply waited until the interruption was over and again turned to me; I finished my answer, and he proceeded with the meeting.

From the start, the board and I worked on shared expectations and a policy of no surprises. Both the board members and I felt comfortable sharing information and often called one another to ensure that everyone was operating from the same base of information. Numerous times, this process alone helped the board weather efforts to divide and conquer it. Board members and I (through the chair) communicated even small and seemingly unimportant details and messages. These were sometimes unimportant, but at other times the apparently trivial became important parts of a puzzle.

Good staff in key positions on the campus were critical to the success of the district during this time. Attempts were made to break into the computer systems, to try the actions of the board in the press, to get student leaders to join the fray, to use requests for public records to bring the system to a halt, to incite unhappy employees to air grievances publicly, to question the actions taken by the board, to challenge the authority of the board to hold closed-session discussions, and to seek confidential information from employees whose job responsibilities involved confidential matters. Most of the college staff responded to the crisis with superb discipline.

Despite this turmoil, students progressed in their education, and outstanding things occurred on the campus. Renovation of major buildings was completed, grant money flowed into the district as never before, the foundation flourished, new partnerships were forged with community agencies, and the next accreditation visit yielded nine major commendations and five recommendations for improvement as part of the reaffirmation for the longest period allowed by our regional accrediting commission.

Board members and the CEO must make themselves available to the community and be willing to address groups—even seemingly hostile groups. One such meeting between two board members and the ministerial alliance resulted in a decision by the ministers to limit support for the dissidents from within the religious communities.

Neither the board nor I responded to the attacks as personal. We avoided showing anger in public. The confidential rights of employees were protected. Perhaps one of the most commendable behavior patterns of the board was that they did not allow leaks or other inappropriate disclosures. Board members understood that they risked personal liability only if they acted outside the legal entity of the board. As long as they acted as a single entity and not as a collection of individuals, they were legally safeguarded.

The college CEO is put into the position to publicly defend and take responsibility for the decision or set of decisions leading up to a crisis, whether or not she is a party to those decisions as they are made. The board bears a similar ultimate responsibility for the actions of its CEO and must stand prepared to defend decisions even when its members do not totally understand the basis for those decisions. For a college to succeed in a participatory system, staff must share the vision and responsibility inherent in participation.

To keep learning alive, one must constantly reinforce learning behaviors that recognize that perfection is never reached. We faced other conflicts at the college and were better prepared and more skilled in some ways. In other ways we reverted to old behavior patterns that were too strong to eliminate with this one instance.

In the end, a leader's role is to remain optimistic, to believe that people are basically good, that caring requires integrity and the strength to make difficult decisions, and that progress can be made. If leaders are to be attracted to these complex jobs and if people with talent and creativity are to lead colleges to achievement that benefits society, every player must proceed in a climate free of violence and with the belief that conflict and civility are not mutually exclusive domains of human endeavor. In an atmosphere of civility, conflict can have productive and creative results. In a hostile environment, both internal and external communities lose the capacity to do good work.

Conflict is seldom rational as it unfolds, but in retrospect, four themes emerged over a three-year period that I believe are instructive for community colleges everywhere.

1. In hiring new leadership, a college may affirm that change is needed at the same time it resists change in favor of traditions and the status quo.
2. The community college boardroom can become the arena for conflicts between values of higher education and values of the community.

3. When there is a threat to the values of higher education from outside the college, those in leadership positions—which in the best case includes the CEO, the board, the faculty, and other staff—all have a stake in defending those values.
4. Change in a college may be strengthened if the college successfully defends its core values in an open conflict.

Following a crisis of such proportion, tensions held in reserve while under siege give way and everyone goes through a period of readjustment. As a result of this experience, I became much more cautious and aware of how any decision, whether it was my decision or that of one of my key administrators, might jeopardize the college. The fine line leaders must walk as they publicly defend actions by staff to whom decisions are delegated involves risk, and one constantly weighs the distinction Argyris made between espoused theory and theory in use (Argyris, 1993, p. 51). Participatory leadership requires greater congruence of values and behaviors between and among college leaders. Community colleges, as a sector of higher education, are in a position to defend environments in which civil discourse and responsible dialogue can inform—even under the most adverse conditions.

References

Argyris, C. (1993). *Knowledge for action.* San Francisco: Jossey-Bass.
Heifetz, R. A. (1996). *Leadership without easy answers.* Cambridge, MA: Belknap Press.
Knox, P. (1997). The campus and the Klan: A classic lesson in civility. *Colorado: Views from CU-Boulder,* 2(3), 10–11.
Wheatley, M. J. (1992). *Leadership and the new science.* San Francisco: Berrett-Koehler.

CHAPTER THREE

Knowing and Influencing the College Culture

Beverly S. Simone

In 1980, I arrived to take the position of director of community and government relations at Milwaukee Area Technical College in Wisconsin. I was the first woman to take a senior position at the college and the youngest member of the president's cabinet. On my first day, I felt I was greeted with the attitude, "You are an outsider." One reason I was treated as an outsider was that the previous administration had been in place for a long time. The existing senior administration had been with the college since 1946—the year I was born. Moreover, the president, who had been at the college since 1967, was still viewed by these insiders as "passing through." I did not represent one of their own. I reasoned that this accounted for their less-than-welcoming reception for me.

The Destructive Power of the College Culture

I do not know how the unrealized assumptions of the senior administration played out during the president's first 13 years, but the aftermath of my hiring and the hiring some months later of another woman for a senior position demonstrated an attitude of incivility and hostility on the part of some senior staff members. When two women were hired in positions that some of the men thought they or another male colleague would receive, the fires within the college were fueled.

Within three months of my hire and the first month after my predecessor's retirement, the president—and ultimately the college—came under repeated attack in the media. This occurred even though this president's work with boards was well respected, and in the year he came under attack, he had become chair of two visible national higher education boards. Because of this commitment, he was away from the college even more than in the past. Although I worked with the president for less than a year, I believe that he felt very strongly that community colleges had a significant voice to share in the higher education world. I saw his passion and vision in wanting to increase the awareness and value of technical education. On campus, however, some administrators and other staff made disparaging remarks about his national leadership. One administrator said, "Those who are doing the real work are never seen as national leaders. They stay at home and tend the fires."

The wife of the president believed and often stated that it was the hiring of women that motivated the media attacks. In my position as community and government relations officer, which included public information and media, I found myself in the midst of the storm. As a newcomer in the community, I had much to learn.

The fires in this college became overwhelming in the midst of continuous daily coverage and heightened investigations of the president, the college, and several other colleges in the state. The president and his family experienced deep personal pain, damaging public coverage, and financial loss. In the end, he was forced to resign. (Subsequently, it appears that the president has chosen never to work again in the public sector of higher education; instead he has become a valuable contributor in private colleges and universities).

Not only was the president under attack, but also the entire board of trustees was dismissed. New trustees were put in place. The state board and the local college districts wrote rules to prevent future actions that might be perceived as questionable by the media and taxpayers. During this time of media inquiry and for several years after, many opportunities for securing funds for students, instructional programs, scholarships, and support services were lost. Furthermore, the college district spent hundreds of thousands of dollars and many staff hours—amounting to even larger sums of money—trying to protect college processes and respond to political pressures.

The charge against the president was serious—"double dipping"; but in the end, no one could resolve that it had actually occurred. The college lost approximately a million dollars in lawyers' fees, investigation, and staff time. Yet, the issue came down to issues such as misreported mileage of 2.2 miles instead of 1.9 miles over a 13-year period. The final disputed amount was approximately $12,000. To many people, this type of expense reporting seemed careless rather than orchestrated for personal gain. Although it is never acceptable to misrepresent miles or any other expenditure of the college, unsubstantiated charges used in a campaign that has at its core the goal of ridding a college of a specific president is a distortion of facts rather than a legitimate case. Did the president actually double-dip or was it simply sloppy accounting? I believe the senior administrators assumed the president considered himself above the rules and therefore set about to work with the media and with external politically minded people to find a way to discredit the president and drive him out.

Some staff members did celebrate their achievement—the president was gone! But did these same individuals consider the long-term consequences of their actions? Did it matter to them that the college, the students, and the community would lose? What was motivating the media coverage, the investigation, and the final actions? What did the president miss in understanding the college culture and working within it to achieve his goals?

As is often the case in this type of media coverage, the college's negative story did not cease with the president's departure. As an interim president was appointed, as a new president was selected, or as any article was written, the questions of leadership were reignited in the media. Legislators used the situation to decrease state support of the technical colleges. The prescribed 36% of funding coming from the state—which had not been honored for a few years—was stricken from statutes. Since then, the amount has eroded to the current status of approximately 19%. In my opinion, the negative media events and the hostility of the senior administrators ultimately led to a devastating loss for the entire college community.

Two concepts that became important to me in terms of leadership strategy were timing and trust. In addition to concentrating on goals and mission, a community college president must consider administrative issues such as how often it is possible to be away from the district without creating negative impressions. A president must strive to remain above reproach by attending to details, especially financial details, in administrative record keeping. If a staff member continues at a meeting when the president leaves, for example, the staff member's budget, rather than the president's budget, should reflect the expenses. Moreover, a significant lesson for me was that initial acts of so-called benign incivility can lead to malignant ends. A simple sarcastic remark such as "I wonder where the president is this week?" repeated over time can have a negative effect on a college's credibility, community support, cohesion among staff, and the reputation of a specific person.

Creating a Progressive Culture at MATC

With this experience in mind, I took my first presidency at Western Wisconsin Technical College (WWTC) in 1987 and then took the presidency at Madison Area Technical College (MATC) in 1989, where I had an opportunity to propose a number of initiatives to enhance civility in the college community by attending to its culture. I believe the president has an important role to play in shaping a college culture, but all people involved with the college can help shape the culture of an organization. The more people feel involved with the college, the more likely they will take an interest in the college environment. A college may have a rich culture that predates the president's arrival. The challenge for a president is to know how to honor that which is core to the organization while attempting to change aspects that keep an organization from becoming the best it can be.

When I arrived at MATC, the college culture was faculty centered, but its administrative leadership was more autocratic in style. The college's departments were loosely formed units that wished to act more autonomously. The college lacked systems and processes for communicating core beliefs and values across the college and to the external communities.

A reporter greeted me on my first day with the question, "How will you shine the light on MATC, when it is in the shadow of the University of Wisconsin and the state capitol?" My vision was to create a participative, inclusive, and diverse culture that encouraged each person to perform to his or her personal best. I believed in the idea that "Together we can lead." I further believed that a more diverse community (in terms of gender, race, ethnicity, sexual orientation, physical abilities, and worldview) within the college could assist in this effort. We lacked diversity in many of our staff classifications and leadership positions; nearly all of those positions were held by White men. We needed to stretch our beliefs and allow other talented people to take leadership roles.

This idea was met with resistance and in some cases with anger. A female president, succeeding a White man with 28 years' tenure, seemed threatening to some members of the long-standing faculty and administrative leadership. Unfounded accusations and rumors of reverse discrimination, including a few failed lawsuits, took center stage as we began to transform the college. To my mind, the need for exposure to new ideas, diversity, and inclusiveness was critical.

To achieve unity and civility within the college, it was important to have a common vision and mission. These needed to be more than legislative mandates or words on paper; they needed to be ways of living that were incorporated into the daily actions of all within the college. I encouraged a process for working within the larger community to develop values, a vision, and a mission. In addition, I initiated steps for staff development to prepare staff for this outreach to broader communities.

Staff Development

As in many organizations in the 1980s, faculty and management were afforded opportunities for development: sabbaticals, in-service programs, workshops, travel, and conferences. Little if any attention was paid, however, to the first-line, or support, staff. MATC support staff, known as paraprofessional and school-related personnel (PSRP), were not invited to hear or participate with the faculty and administration on key issues before the college. Marginal representation in regional accreditation was an exception.

My administration put initial processes in place whereby PSRP could be partners within the college's leadership. An early strategy was to invite the presidents of both the faculty and PSRP along with the senior administrators to become members of the president's cabinet, a strategy I had initiated successfully two years earlier at WWTC. The strategy created an opportunity for the formal leadership to work in preparation for board meetings, to serve as final approval for programs and budgets, and to discuss and resolve or delegate major organizational issues.

My colleagues, who had been experienced in pro forma unionized collective bargaining settings, were curious as to how senior administrators could sit at the same table and discuss administrative actions, board policies, and strategic planning with union leadership. Defining clear ground rules and purposes for the group helped. Today many more colleges are using this inclusive strategy for formal leaders within a union environment. In the mid-1980s it was a rare practice, and I was fortunate to work with union presidents who shared a commitment to the students and to the greater good of the college. We implemented win–win or interest-based bargaining techniques and practices to ensure issue resolution, and we created an ongoing union and management team to resolve issues outside of formal negotiations.

Some of the staff development activities we incorporated early at MATC included continuous improvement, Covey training, critical thinking, and diversity training. To create a continuous improvement or quality improvement culture, we could not just deal with the quantitative aspects of the work. Qualitative assessments were also needed. I believe these staff development strategies helped to build trust, commitment, and inspiration among the staff, which in turn promoted an atmosphere of respect and civility.

Valuing and Promoting Diversity

Early in our commitment to staff development, the MATC administration also had to cope with a new exposure to the value of diversity. Wisconsin has strong northern European roots and a very small population of people of color. Madison, known as a liberal city, is still challenged with issues of racial and ethnic diversity. MATC is but a microcosm of the state and city. Achieving more racial and ethnic diversity at MATC took awareness, education, and changes in systems and practices. Working with staff of color, I wrote the following statement, which became the foundation for subsequent college actions:

Commitment to Diversity

MATC's response to the changing nature of diversity, which goes beyond categories such as gender, race, and disability, requires a commitment by each member of the MATC community to create and sustain a learning environment built on respect for the unique experiences and potential of all. This ensures that MATC is preparing students personally and professionally to become active and successful participants in a complex, diverse world.

I initiated a series of conversations and follow-up with community leaders from the four predominant racial groups within the district. Sensitive and credible national speakers were invited to staff development days. Opportunities for small-group discussion of staff members' beliefs and fears were provided in conjunction with substantive information. Working with external consultants, my administrative team developed a Train the Trainer Diversity Education Series for the college and included the training of faculty, PSRP, and managers to deliver training across the college in the broader construct of diversity.

MATC staff participated in the diversity seminars, and all new staff members knew that participation in the training was a requirement. The Intercultural Council was formed to monitor the activities and results of the college related to the broad issues of diversity. In 1996, MATC was recognized by the governor with the Breaking of the Glass Ceiling award and by NAACP and EEOC for achieving diversification of staff and students within the college. During this work to create a diverse culture within the college, we began to identify core values for the college. Early dialogues with all staff planted the seeds that grew into the accepted core values of diversity. These core values were later identified and articulated as part of our community-wide strategic planning process. They included a commitment to excellence, continuously improving the quality of work; respect, recognizing the essential dignity of every person; and integrity, acting truthfully and following through.

Shared Strategic Plan

An important step in creating a more inclusive, participatory, and diverse culture within MATC was the creation of a community-based strategic plan. As most presidents know, there is a lack of coordination between planning and budgeting in many organizations. Although we say the words "continuous planning and resource allocation," in reality we often see that budgets are based on past practices, biases, percentages, or unspoken agreements rather than the highest priorities of the college's mission and vision. To address this cultural challenge within MATC, we conducted a district-wide strategic planning process that engaged all members of the board of trustees and representative members of MATC management, faculty, and PSRP with external community members. Participating in a two-and-a-half-day workshop to create the strategic direction for the college were 170 people, including employers, legislators, labor unions, current and prospective students, other higher education representatives, elected officials, community leaders, grassroots advocates, and MATC representatives

We were careful to build on our past and our history of quality programs and services while acknowledging the impossibility of "being all things for all people." The results of this shared dialogue were a revised mission statement for the college, a vision statement, five strategic directions, and increased community buy-in for the college's programs and services. To further promote cross-college dialogue within MATC college teams, Strategic Initiative Excellence Teams (SIETs) were created to provide leadership for each of the five strategic directions. The college had five vice presidents, and each one was appointed to serve as a member of a SIET in which she or he did not have operational authority. Although the vice presidents were anxious initially, this responsibility created a deeper understanding of the totality of the college work that cut across functional lines. Although far from perfect, this system worked for five years and was celebrated as we continued our journey in improvement with a revised organizational structure.

College Values at Work

One of the college's strategic initiatives was improving the organizational climate. Because this area was not closely tied to any functional unit but truly affected the entire college, SIET was authorized to do operational work and identify the college's core values and develop implementation strategies. The core values of excellence, respect, and integrity were communicated within the college. College documents, including business cards, communicated these values. Evaluation tools used for staff performance incorporated questions and guidelines for assessing a staff member's demonstration of the values. New staff orientation provided an opportunity for the college president to discuss the importance of these values and to encourage staff to check the alignment with their own values.

Although we would have liked to have seen everyone demonstrating all the values all the time, we realized that we were a learning college and that people's behaviors would develop over time. It is critical that college presidents and CEOs model the desired behavior and acknowledge the times we fail to speak or act most appropriately. Our daily interactions with others should set the tone and create the atmosphere embodied by the college's values. In addition, we should be open to having 360-degree evaluations completed on ourselves by our boards, direct reports, and other appropriate colleagues across the college.

MATC has provided Values at Work sessions for functional units. Small groups such as the research and planning team or the instructional deans worked with outside facilitators to create meaning for how the institutional values work within their own unit. Participants explored how they as individuals have demonstrated the college values. They identified times when the values had not been practiced and how they as a unit and as individuals could take concrete actions to better live the values within their unit in the future.

Other systems and processes at MATC were modified based on the college's values. The recruitment and selection process for all employees communicated the values. During interviews candidates were asked to speak to situations in which they had to demonstrate excellence, respect, and integrity. The employee performance assessments incorporated questions related to these three values and learning college principles.

Learning College Principles

In addition to the three core values, MATC's vision of Leader in Learning ascribed additional principles by which staff should live. As a follow-up, all staff were invited and expected to participate in dialogues regarding how their work related to the learning college principles. Dialogue sessions were scheduled around the clock so that it was convenient for all staff to become engaged. One of the board members volunteered for the midnight to 2:00 a.m. session to demonstrate commitment to employees. Some helpful data-gathering instruments for understanding the organizational culture include the Personnel Assessment of College Environment (PACE) instrument and the Student Assessment of the

College Environment (SACE) measurement. By comparing data over the years, we identified trends and areas of growth as well as areas for improvement.

Recommendations for Encouraging a Positive Culture

To develop a positive culture within a college, time must be spent to develop systems for addressing students' issues. Conflicts can arise among students, between students and faculty or staff, or between students and the college as an entity. Community colleges strive to be student centered. They must therefore keep learning at the forefront and realize that sources of conflict and crises in a student's life will have a negative impact on learning. College leaders must set the tone about the importance of addressing and, it is hoped, resolving students' conflicts.

A good beginning is to ask questions regarding the college's current methodology for monitoring student-related disputes. These disputes may include student code of conduct concerns, grade disagreements, interpersonal conflicts, discrimination or harassment allegations, and nonacademic grievances. At MATC we found that our past practices were allowing too many conflicts to escalate beyond the first and easiest-to-address stage. Therefore, we decided to invest in creating a comprehensive conflict management response unit. The one-stop shop had the responsibility and authority to deal with student-related conflicts. Anyone at the college—students, faculty, and staff—could bring issues to the conflict management unit if the conflict involved students.

An important goal for this type of service area is to increase students' and staff's knowledge of conflict management strategies, and one of the first concepts is self-responsibility. Students and faculty working with unit staff learn more effective communication, assertiveness, and decision-making skills. Using these enhanced skills, both students and faculty discover that most conflicts can be handled in a fair and reasonable manner.

It is also important to have clear, well-documented, and frequently communicated college policies and procedures that protect the rights, while clarifying the responsibilities, of college community members. Appropriate behaviors cannot be enforced if students and staff do not know what the expected behaviors are. Policies and procedures such as the student code of conduct should be published in the student handbook or catalog and made available on the college's official Web site. The student code of conduct should include procedures on appeals, records, probation, dismissal, and suspension.

Intervention Resources

Intervention resources available to students and staff also assist early resolution of conflicts. Some examples of intervention resources include the following:

- academic advising and counseling
- specialized workshops on time and stress management and on study skills
- child care
- alcohol and other drug abuse prevention programs
- intercultural student access and support
- disability resource services

College leaders who recognize the importance of establishing and maintaining conflict management services will see results. These services and intervention resources interrupt the crisis life cycle so that the crisis is either avoided or does not escalate. At MATC we implemented the one-stop center and intervention strategies. Although the number of cases did not decline, we were better equipped to interrupt the cycle and work more effectively to resolve conflicts. Consequently, students and staff could spend more time learning.

■ ■ ■

I believe that if college leaders work to preserve that which is good and continue to improve the culture, we have a better chance of avoiding crises and episodes and attitudes of incivility or at least of addressing them in an effective and healthful manner. Of course, there are many acts of incivility that even the most effective president cannot proactively prevent or effectively manage. As Margaret Mead (1935) observed in her conclusion of *Sex and Temperament in Three Primitive Societies*, "If we are to achieve a richer culture, rich in contrasting values, we must recognize the whole gamut of human potentialities, and so weave a less arbitrary social fabric, one in which each diverse human gift will find a fitting place."

References

Mead, M. (1935). *Sex and temperament in three primitive societies.* New York: HarperCollins.

CHAPTER FOUR

Compassionate Leadership Transcending Prejudice

Zelema Harris

The Importance of Social Capital

I grew up in a close and supportive Black community in Liberty, Texas, during the 1940s and 1950s that experienced numerous incidents of discrimination by White people. In fact, I grew up with the impression that White people were nearly always brutal and rarely compassionate. Yet my Black community instilled in me not resentment or fear, but a strong commitment to showing respect, kindness, and compassion toward all people. As an adult, my views broadened and I learned that civility, like brutality, is not an attitude confined to one group or race. Civility is engendered and learned. I carry the spirit of Liberty with me, and I have tried to apply its civil and compassionate principles as a community college leader.

Mistreatment of others and an overall lack of civility have been major concerns of mine throughout my life. As children in the all-Black grade school in East Texas, we pledged allegiance to the flag, we sang patriotic songs, and Black soldiers from our community died in wars fought in foreign lands. Yet here in the United States, Blacks were denied even the most basic of civil rights. I recall a time when I was eight years old, when I had to stand on a piece of paper while my mother drew an outline of my foot. Black people were not allowed to try on shoes in the White community nearly seven miles away.

My mother was an expert at helping her five children avoid contact with White people. I did not make it easy for her, however. When I was 12 years old, I slipped away from her at the A&P Store and drank from the Whites-only water fountain. The store manager spotted me and started walking in my direction. My mother, recognizing the danger, yanked me away from the water fountain and scolded me. I was not offended by my mother's action because I knew she was trying to protect me from a more severe punishment from the store manager.

No matter what happened to me in the White world, I always experienced a sense of joy when I returned to my own community. In the Black community,

I was encouraged by teachers who took me to my first play and told me that I could become anything I wanted to be. My brothers and sisters taught me to read and write by the time I was four. These acts and many others were the gifts of my community. The socialization of a Black child in two different worlds may seem incomprehensible, but it was a way of life for me and for many Black Americans.

The children in my generation were expected to attend college or to receive some type of vocational training, and most did. Liberty Community School, located in Newton County, Texas, was responsible for training teachers, architects, engineers, nurses, musicians, nutritionists, and other professionals during my generation in the 1940s and 1950s. Political scientist Robert Putnam, author of *Bowling Alone: The Collapse and Revival of American Community* (2000), would have described our community as having "social capital." In a 1995 lecture sponsored by the American Political Science Association, Putnam defined social capital as "features of social life—networks, norms, and trust—that enable participants to act together more effectively to pursue shared objectives" (Putnam, 1995, p. 665).

The social capital in Liberty allowed us to grow and develop as healthy human beings, despite the obstacles. We were never taught that we were victims. In fact, we were taught that we could compete with anyone, and much of our education and training were geared toward competing within White America. These strong moral convictions and intolerance for injustice have permeated my approach to leading. In fact, my experiences as a child have shaped every aspect of my life.

My father, who was born in 1866, was 73 when I was born. His mother was a slave. After slavery was abolished, she stayed on the property of the slave master and reared her three children, including my father. As an adult, he worked as a carpenter and farmer. Although he never learned to read or write, my father taught me three of the most important lessons in life: acceptance, respect, and unconditional love. My mother taught me that freedom was within. She had a saying that I heard most of my life: "Get your education, and nobody can take it away."

My mother also taught me about showing compassion for others. I cannot recall a time while growing up when someone was not living with us. Generally, it was some relative who was out of work, or as my mother would say, "temporarily down on their luck." I remember when three children lived with us for over several months. My mother prepared all the meals and completed other household chores for eight children.

My early experiences with White America were not positive and led me to distrust all Whites. Ironically, it was one of my White professors at the University of Kansas (UK) who helped me to bridge the two worlds—the nurturing one in which I grew up and the external hostile world. He encouraged me to use my voice in the White world. He taught me that justice was stronger than fear. He was the first White person I knew who was compassionate.

During my years at UK and subsequently at the Metropolitan Community Colleges in Kansas City, Missouri, I worked for and was mentored by some very talented and caring people who reinforced my belief that bosses can be kind and supportive and still expect high performance from employees. I have discovered that compassion is the common denominator shared by the most effective leaders. It is the one tool that has served me best over the 35 years during which I have held leadership positions.

I have used the lessons my parents and others taught me to lead institutions through times of difficult change. Early in my professional career my beliefs about kindness and compassion were more personal and I was able to demonstrate them through one-on-one interactions, conversations, and speeches. Later in my professional career, as I experienced more incivility in the workplace, I used my leadership position to institutionalize concepts that would create respectful dissent, respect for and understanding of diversity, and accountability for our own actions, all of which are imbedded in a number of programs that have been implemented at Parkland College, discussed later in this chapter.

Ground Rules for Fostering Civility in Academe

When I was in graduate school, I worked full-time in the admissions office. During that time, I learned a lesson about the use of kindness that has worked well for me over the years. One of the unit managers was notorious for making unkind remarks to his subordinates. I had heard stories about how he brought people to tears and how his employees feared him. Although I did not report directly to this manager, he called me in one day to discuss a decision I had made about the awarding of transfer credits.

Although I was afraid, I resolved not to allow fear to control me. I decided that I would treat the manager with respect and kindness. By the time I left his office, he had accepted my explanation for the decision I had made, and we discussed a number of other issues affecting the awarding of credit for international students. Perhaps I was lucky, but my strategy seemed to work in this case. What struck me as even more important than his civil response to my civility, however, was the lack of any institutional policy or system in place to address this manager's generally unacceptable behavior.

What is the best way to address incivility in an institutional setting? Civility is more than being nice. Civility requires the setting of ground rules regarding public discourse. Before meeting with the graduate school manager, I set some rules for myself: Along with showing kindness and respect, I would not be intimidated, and I would address only the issue at hand.

When I became a community college president more than 20 years ago, personal values and civility were not commonly discussed in the workplace. As long as a worker got the job done, it did not matter how he or she treated co-workers and subordinates. If a worker complained about a manager to someone in the administration, the worker was told to learn how to get along. Occasionally, a manager who verbally abused subordinates might get a slap on the wrist, but the blame was almost always pointed at the complaining worker for being too sensitive. Seldom, if ever, were managers or other employees held accountable for their mistreatment of others.

As institutional leaders, we must find ways to create conditions in which employees and students can address issues of public interest, no matter how controversial. According to the key findings in the Penn National Commission on Society, Culture and Community (2000),

> "public talk" plays a central role in the functioning of a well-ordered democratic society and can facilitate productive dialogue on such "hot button" issues as immigration, race, abortion, and affirmative action. The processes of engaged, productive public discourse de-sensitize such issues and facilitate co-existence, even in the face of frank opinions and irresolvable disagreements.

Civility in academe, then, is the ability to address these topics within the framework of respect for one another's opinions. This type of civility demands that education leaders come to a discussion with the idea that we are willing to change our minds. Simply being nice, although important, may not move the organization forward if it is the only skill used in our day-to-day interactions.

Although some scholars believe that incivility is on the rise and cite evidence to support their claims, Judith Rodin, president of the University of Pennsylvania, counters that "incivility is nothing new. It is really a continuation of behaviors that have always been with us but have more impact now because they are more observable. The economics of the media have really transformed the opportunity for and, indeed, the promotion of incivility because it sells well" (Freiberg, 2000). Television talk show hosts, for example, are known for encouraging boorish, loud behavior among guests. If the guests are not sufficiently obnoxious, the hosts may say something incendiary to ignite a reaction that will entertain the audience.

In her thought-provoking book *All About Love*, bell hooks chastised the mass media for dwelling on and perpetuating "an ethic of domination and violence because our image makers have more intimate knowledge of these realities than they have with the realities of love" (2000, p. 95). I agree that people cannot help but be affected and shaped by the images of violence, rudeness, and cruelty that dominate popular television, movies, and popular music. One approach is to try to avoid individuals who are rude and abusive. Avoiding them, however, in a way supports the negative behavior and allows other people to continue to be subjected to it.

When I first arrived at Parkland in 1990, I was looking for ways to get to know the college. I held open forums where people were encouraged to attend and ask questions about the college's future. After one of these forums, I received an angry letter from a long-time faculty member. He was concerned about the direction in which I was leading the college. He accused me of "planting" people in the audience to ask questions related to inclusiveness and institutional transformation. The letter concluded with a prediction that I would soon be run off the campus.

The "angry faculty letter" incident occurred at the same time Parkland was organizing its first Leadership Development Seminar. I made sure the unhappy faculty member was one of only 20 faculty and staff invited to participate in the seminar. On the last day of the seminar, the faculty member who had written the letter predicting what he hoped would be my short-term presidential tenure stood up in front of the group and said, "I have taught at this college for more than 20 years. This is the first time that I've felt somebody cared about me." By engaging this disaffected individual, our college was, in essence, creating its own version of what Putnam defined as social capital. Engaged students learn more, and faculty and staff who are involved in leading the college will be more creative in addressing institutional challenges (Putnam, 2000, pp. 18–19). When I have used this situation as a case study in teaching graduate students in community college leadership, I have been heartened by how the students suggested resolving the matter. Invariably, their solution was to engage the disgruntled faculty member in a dialogue to learn more about his concerns.

Civility Starts at the Top

In *Civility: Manners, Morals, and the Etiquette of Democracy*, Carter (1998), a law professor at Yale, wrote that civility "is the sum of the many sacrifices we are called to make for the sake of living together." Carter's eloquent quote can be extended to the workplace, where we spend so many hours of our lives, and it suggests that one cause of incivility is an unwillingness to make sacrifices. How, then, does one build civility in an academic environment? It begins with the college CEO. CEOs must be clear in both their vision and their actions that incivility will not be tolerated under any circumstances, and they must model civility.

Training classes, workshops, discussion groups, and other opportunities for engagement need to be planned and implemented on campus. These efforts are necessary, partly because there is no law against management abuse. Management abuse can be defined as the misuse of authority and power to intimidate or exclude individual workers. I support equal opportunity, but not when it comes to harassment, rudeness, and uncivil behavior. It may not be a crime to abuse employees and students, but that does not make this behavior acceptable. More important, it does not foster a productive, supportive workplace. The Web site www.workingwounded.com and other outlets such as the Dilbert cartoon strip provide a comical view of bosses, co-workers, and other job-related war stories. The underlying message is a sad one, however: Too many of our employees are hurt, angry, humiliated, uninspired, and even scared.

Promoting Civility at Parkland

A recent study by the graduate business school at the University of North Carolina (Pearson, 2000) illustrates the impact of incivility on an institution's bottom line:

- 28% of study participants lost work time in trying to avoid the instigator of the uncivil behavior.
- 53% lost work time worrying about the incident or what might happen next.
- 37% reported that they felt less committed to their organization.
- 46% thought about changing jobs to get away from the situation.
- 12% changed jobs in order to avoid the instigator.

Parkland has taken several steps toward building a civil, compassionate campus. Early efforts were facilitated when the North Central Association (NCA), Parkland's accrediting institution, issued its Statement on Access, Equity, and Diversity in 1991. As part of the accreditation process,

The commission expects an institution to create and maintain a teaching and learning environment that supports sensitivity to diverse individuals and groups. Furthermore, the commission expects an affiliated institution to discourage acts of racism, sexism, bigotry, and violence and to place in proper perspective the differences that separate and the commonalities that bind all peoples and cultures.

In 1992, I appointed a committee on Access, Equity, and Cultural Diversity at Parkland. The committee was charged with developing an institutional response to the NCA Statement on Access, Equity, and Diversity and to create a long-range plan for addressing these issues. Several significant actions resulted from the committee's work. One of the most important was the committee's presentation in 1993 of a cultural diversity resolution that was unanimously passed by Parkland's student government, the Parkland College Association (open to all faculty, staff, and administrators), and Parkland's board of trustees. Diversity needed to be infused in everything we do at Parkland, from learning more about diverse cultures to student support services.

It also was important to make more concerted efforts to hire diverse faculty. In 1997, the board of directors issued a resolution calling for an action plan to increase diversity among full-time faculty at the college. The fact that no racial minority serves on Parkland's elected board of trustees makes this decision even more significant. Today, much of the committee's work continues through Parkland's Center for Excellence in Teaching and Learning. The center initiated a classroom assessment and research initiative called Culture Care, in which faculty assess the hidden curriculum or barriers to learning for diverse students. Another workshop is called Connecting Cultures in the Classroom: Reaching Each Student. These faculty-led efforts not only promote civility, they help create a more nurturing environment for all learners.

The last statement in Parkland's Mission and Purposes pledges "to provide a nurturing, quality work environment for all college personnel." This statement seemed more like wishful thinking than reality after I had read several human resources office reports on harassment claims, disputes between supervisors and employees, and other unsettling workplace incidents. Something tangible was needed to make the campus a "nurturing, quality work environment."

That something tangible became the "Leading the Respectful Workplace" training series, in which employees learn what constitutes sexual harassment, discrimination, and management abuse. The workshops are intended to teach managers more than what is legal and what is illegal, however. The main objective is to create a work environment in which every employee feels respected and safe. Invitations and announcements of the various training and learning opportunities typically are communicated college-wide via e-mail.

Parkland's faculty-driven Center for Excellence in Teaching and Learning offers a variety of activities that promote civility in the classroom and in every corner of the campus. Although the majority of learning opportunities focus on faculty and student issues, the center also co-facilitates training with the counseling center, the human resources department, and other areas of the college. All employees, faculty or staff, are welcome and encouraged to attend the center's offerings. The center's workshops have included a discussion on service learning. One could argue convincingly that the classroom is a good place for students to start developing a sense of civic responsibility. Service learning provides students with practical ways to put their civic responsibility into action.

An institution's leadership sets the tone, creates the culture, and brings the college's values to life. Nearly 200 faculty and staff have attended the annual Parkland Leadership Development Seminar, which began in 1994. The success of this effort has made me an enthusiastic proponent of the grow-your-own approach to leadership development. The curriculum of the leadership seminar includes nuts-and-bolts topics such as budget issues. But it is the less tangible information that gives meaning to our everyday work. Participants at the leadership seminar also have the opportunity to take the Myers–Briggs assessment and to examine their own leadership styles. In one session, they role-play specific workplace situations and difficult employee issues. During the discussion that takes place after the role-playing, participants see that their individual choices and responses affect other human beings. This is a responsibility not only of being a leader but also of living and working in a civil society. Musician Carlos Santana hopes for a world where we have "a passion for compassion" (cited in Fong-Torres, 2003, p. 5). Our colleges should, too. They should be places of transformation. If we truly want a more civil society, let it begin with us, as compassionate leaders.

References

Carter, S. L. (1998). *Civility: Manners, morals, and the etiquette of democracy.* New York: Basic Books.

Fong-Torres, B. (2003). He wails for the world. *Parade* (March 30).

Freiberg, P. (2000). Butting heads, American style. *Monitor on Psychology* (May).

hooks, b. (2000). *All about love: New visions.* New York: Morrow.

Pearson, C. (2000). *Workplace "incivility" study.* Chapel Hill, NC: University of North Carolina, Kenan-Flagler Business School. Available from http://bullyinginstitute.org/home/twd/bb/res/pearson.html

Penn National Commission on Society, Culture and Community. (2000). *Key findings of the Penn National Commission.* Available from http://www.upenn.edu/pnc/keyfindings.html

Putnam, R. D. (1995). Tuning in, tuning out: The strange disappearance of social capital in America. *PS* (December), 664–683.

Putnam, R. D. (2000). *Bowling alone: The collapse and revival of American community.* New York: Simon & Schuster.

CHAPTER FIVE

Addressing Challenges to Civility on Campus

Paul A. Elsner

Emerging education leaders may suppose that a considerate, civil, and respectful attitude will naturally characterize college discourse and relationships. Indeed, colleges and universities encourage a language of inquiry and dissent in an open and forthright discussion of issues. An important tenet of the academic system is free speech and open discussion, and upholding academic freedom is a principle to which community college leaders adhere.

Challenges to Civility

Unfortunately, forms of incivility do arise in college and university settings. Manifestations of it include a tendency to attack those in positions of leadership, as well as peer-to-peer incivility among faculty, staff, and students, who may become victims of hurtful and inconsiderate styles of discourse.

Devaluing the Leadership

Critics of a college's leadership may attempt to devalue the leaders in the eyes of the college community and the public. Because administrators are well paid and voluntarily accept the administrative positions, people may feel that they should anticipate and handle the stresses and tensions that go with these positions. Attacks, however, may become part of a political power game rather than a discourse based on a legitimate difference of views. For example, union leaders may claim that it is the leader's responsibility to find money to support programs and salaries. Thus the leader may be blamed and held in contempt for not delivering on the demands.

When boards of trustees hire college presidents, they almost always have the support of both the incoming and outgoing faculty senate presidents, many of whom worked closely with each other to recommend a particular candidate to the board. Even mild objections to an appointment—from either faculty senate presidents or members of screening committees—would cause most boards or chancellors to decline the appointment. In many cases, the entire screening committee is delighted with the candidate, going so far as to reaffirm the successful candidate's philosophy and goals during interviews. Such screening committee affirmation may not effectively translate to the other segments of the college community, however, which can result in a disparity between the screening process and the implementation process. A candidate may think, "I am doing exactly what I am expected to do from the standpoint of the compact reached with the screeners," and thus appear ignorant of or even offensive toward the larger college community.

Explanations for lack of support for the leadership are varied. One reason may be that issues under debate are not always clear. Faculty, for example, may not want to tackle a muddled issue, nor do they want to be caught between issues. Such avoidance leaves only a handful of power-oriented groups to press issues through and to breach democratic processes, causing further discontent among employees. Another possible reason for lack of support is fear of retaliation in dealing with an openly raucous group or person. One may risk job security or loss of previously granted favors in a department, such as good schedules or favorite class sections.

In seeking to remain objective, CEOs may be criticized for not siding with a particular group, and CEOs often do not encourage lateral censure because it could cause division on the campus, with even more serious negative consequences. Usually, all CEOs can do is wade in where trouble lies and hope to emerge intact; allowing faculty or other employees to battle one another is unwise and potentially dangerous.

Questions of Power and Authority

To some employees, power might mean protection. In the case of the Maricopa district, for example, Rio Salado Community College illustrated this by bending its rule to use no more than 10% adjunct faculty. Full-time faculty probably felt a loss of power, sensing that they could be replaced. In addition, the rule bending slowed Rio's ability to hire full-time faculty who would provide buffers for faculty with seniority—in other words, newly hired faculty who would go first in the event of layoffs. In California, the legislature attempted to write matters of faculty power into statutes by passing pro-faculty bills. California prescribed governance features that colleges were required by law to honor.

The question remains: Who should run a community college? Boards think they have a public mandate; some faculty members may believe that all quality and related professional conduct should rest in their hands. It should be no surprise, then, that anger and other unrest can occur. In some ways, it is amazing they do not emerge more often.

Votes of No Confidence

Several community college CEOs believe they have been subjected to poorly justified votes of no confidence. Seasoned administrators also can suffer such censures. Discussions of this trend have occurred at meetings of the AACC Presidents Academy meetings, the League for Innovation, and at RC-2000 and other gatherings of community college leaders board meetings.

In some cases, votes of no confidence may be justified. Faculty, in particular, may feel helpless to remedy a situation or correct bad administrative behavior, and such votes may be their only recourse. The most serious effect, however, is the damage that can result when a mere handful of people orchestrates censures without appropriate discussion and involvement of the general faculty. Sometimes only a subcommittee of a faculty senate is needed to issue public pronouncement; other times, the entire faculty senate, but not the entire faculty, is included. Only occasionally, but not frequently enough, the entire faculty is required to be thoroughly briefed on the issues surrounding a vote of no confidence.

Board Conflicts

If faculty may be reluctant to laterally censure inappropriate behavior of peers, the same holds true for boards of trustees. Even board members admit that some are more oriented toward their constituency than board unity. Although most board members do divest their allegiances over time and become more broadly motivated, some elected members may feel loyalty both to the board and to those who helped elect them.

It can be very painful for CEOs or other administrators to fend off false impressions—including blatant character destruction—when a new board member is elected who carries into the office false information about the CEO. Ideally, disputing parties should meet to resolve misunderstandings before challenges to a public servant are aired in front of a public audience. In Dr. Romero's case, for example, there was evidence of the board both splitting and unifying to preserve the college's integrity.

In one case I know of, a press release described a board member's actions, including involvement in his own certification of the board of accountants. A faculty member openly attacked the author of the press release, mentioning the board member's lapse of certification. Although the board member had not intentionally misrepresented himself, the attacking person publicly accused him through a 10,000-person e-mail distribution list. This attack was unwarranted, for it did not take into account that the board member's setbacks resulted from serious illness in his family, to which he had turned all or most of his attention. He also had health problems of his own. His loss of certification was not a matter of either his character or his professional competence. To the contrary, this board member was competent and happened to support and contribute to a number of charitable causes. He did not deserve such uncivil e-mail broadcasts from an ill-advised person.

Misuse of Electronic Communication

As illustrated in the preceding example, although e-mail technology may enhance communication on a campus, it also provides a powerful vehicle for promoting negative personal agendas. College communities have attempted to guide the conduct of e-mail use, but because of legal and practical reasons for allowing e-mail to be an open communication system, most regulations concentrate on concerns such as system (hardware) integrity, business etiquette, and system overload. Such guidelines may not elaborate on the larger issues of ethics and civility.

In the earlier stages of e-mail use at the Maricopa colleges, the system wanted to encourage use of e-mail as a new innovation and felt that curtailing its use would destroy motivation. The vice chancellor for information technology reported that much struggle and bewilderment accompanied abuse regulation, however. Abuse ranged from advertisements of "rent my RV" to "buy my puppy dogs." Only one of the many restrictions listed in the Maricopa guidelines under "computing resource standards" specifically referred to personal abuses such as discrediting individuals, hateful language, or breaches of civility (see Appendix B).

One eastern community college district had close to a 24-year history of experiencing a steady flow of anonymous letters that spread false information and dangerous rumors. Long-standing college community members had learned to endure these letters. When a young CEO replaced the retiring president, however, the letters became intolerable. Within two years, the new president resigned and moved into private industry. Regrettably, higher education lost an outstanding leader, who subsequently has done extremely well in the private sector.

I once encountered a person who used the e-mail system to advance his criticism of a college administration as well as the policies of his own department.

Although some of his criticisms may have been valid and I found some of his witticisms humorous, I considered his missives inappropriate because he openly belittled people by name and offered long homilies, essays, and diatribes by e-mail. This form of communication easily leads to misunderstandings, allowing the potential for destructive personal attacks without appropriate opportunity for response; this is a serious misuse of the technology that needs an injection of civility.

Environments That May Foster Aggression

Certain conditions on campus may tend to foster incivility among the staff or community. Environments vulnerable to incivility include the following:

CEO's absence or failure to set boundaries. In this case, hurtful, disrespectful interactions, abuse over territory, gossiping, or unethical standards may go unchecked.

Absence of codes of behavior. Faculty, staff, and boards of trustees should adhere to prescribed codes of behavior. These codes should be debated and formally adopted as a doctrine that bonds the culture to an appropriate civility, even in the face of possible heated engagement. To include the students, their councils of government should be brought into the discussion. Students can feel personally attacked over disputed campus matters. Student learners should be assisted in designing workplace and fair conduct codes for their review and possible adoption.

Detachment from the community. Staff, faculty, and students may describe an offending party in the third person rather than a component of the larger community: "The faculty are acting up again," or "The crafts unit has angered the director of operations." We seldom say "we" have a problem. It is always "they" or "them."

Fear of peer retaliation or censure. Faculty and staff members may dislike a colleague's behavior but fear speaking out. Peer retaliation can be politically costly; therefore, faculty and staff may choose to keep silent and endure.

Aggressive expression can increase stress levels and even cause serious illness among colleagues and supervisors. It accelerates the demise of a college environment; the leadership might overlook its early symptoms, as attacks are made against persons rather than the merit of an argument. An individual crusade, at first not totally serious, may grow until the person believes "I am right; therefore, anything I say or any degree of harm I cause is justified."

Civility Versus Freedom of Expression in an Academic Setting

A decline in civility can affect learning and teaching as well as the quality of life on a college campus. Issues of cultural diversity, codes of behavior, and free speech may collide in the broad endeavor to create a diverse, vibrant, and healthful community of learning.

Attempts at Speech Codes

Courts of law have not looked favorably on efforts by universities to curtail expression by means of speech codes. Stanford University, the University of Wisconsin, and the University of Michigan, for example, were turned down by courts when they attempted to establish speech codes.

In 2002, Harvard University designated The Committee on Healthy University, a panel of six faculty member, six students, and three law school staff members, to prepare speech code recommendations to bring before the Harvard faculty. An article in the Arizona Republic (Peter 2002) describes the debate that ensued when Harvard's law school announced its consideration of a ban on offensive speech:

> The speech-code proposal has stirred an intense internal debate about the commitment to freedom of expression at a school whose illustrious alumni have helped define the nation's free speech rights. Some are wondering whether a campus renowned for its bare-knuckled, confrontational style of teaching is getting a little touchy-feely.
>
> "What I do find amazing is that it should be considered at a law school, any law school, because one thing that law schools do is study the Constitution and these codes are clearly in violation of the First Amendment," said Harvey Silvergate, a Harvard Law graduate and civil liberties litigator.

The article pointed out that some supporters of speech harassment bans nonetheless express concern for and interest in protecting the cornerstone First Amendment: Members of the Black Law Students Association, which called for the policy, say it is possible to curb chronically offensive behavior without infringing on the First Amendment.

Classroom Behavior

A paper presented by Robert L. Heinemann at the 82nd SCA Annual Convention in San Diego (November, 1996) suggested that acts of incivility in the classroom are increasing. Heinemann cited the following student behaviors:

> The degree of incivility varies, but there seems to be a general agreement that it is on the rise. According to Monagham (1995), "bored" students simply get up in the middle of a lecture and leave; some simply read the paper. Monagham also reports incidents of a student challenging a teacher to a fight over a grade, of a student calling her teacher a "bitch" in a class, and of classes becoming so unruly that teachers are simply forced to leave. Racial epithets still are heard at our nation's most exclusive schools (p. 3).

Kuhlenschmidt and Layne (1999, pp. 45–47) have said that difficult behavior includes "stalking, intimidation, physical or verbal attacks and 'hijacking' classrooms." Kuhlenschmidt and Layne (p. 46) stress several steps and postures for confronting incivility in the classroom and offer strategies for dealing with difficult behavior. These strategies vary from weighing the situation carefully before jumping in with a solution to assessing the teacher's own behavior. According to Kuhlenschmidt and Layne, the source of the problem may not be simple to trace. The authors recommend addressing these basic questions:

- What is the behavior? What is the situation?
- When does it happen?
- What occurs before, during, and after the behavior?
- Who is involved or affected?
- What degree of harm to the student or to others is being involved?
- How do you feel about the behavior?
- What remedies or changes does the situation call for? (pp. 46-48)

These questions are not easy to answer, but Kuhlenschmidt and Layne place value in sorting out as many aspects of the uncivil behavior as possible. Hasty decisions can exacerbate the undesirable behaviors.

Some uncivil behavior can emerge without the faculty member being aware of its development. Tiberius and Flak (1999) distinguished subtle behaviors from the more evident classroom incivility discussed above:

Incivility is speech or action that is disrespectful or rude. Incivility in the contemporary classroom may include insulting and even violent behavior. In the one-to-one teaching and learning situation, by contrast, such extreme forms of incivility are rarely manifested. To the casual observer even dysfunctional dyads may appear pleasant. Typically the teacher and learner smile, laugh, and converse politely. The teacher does not have to contend with disruptive outbursts from the back of the room or dominant speakers who are threatening to take over the group. . . . [W]e argue that the overt civility of dyadic relationships can mask unexpressed tensions and that these tensions, if not addressed, can increase to the explosive point, at which the relationship itself is destroyed (p. 3).

Some teachers use a bantering, challenging style of classroom management. A class may resonate to the give-and-take of the creative tension that a gifted teacher can facilitate, but a student could feel threatened and personally devalued by such an environment if the class—which may enjoy the humor or fun of a situation—overlooks the isolation or hurt feelings of a student. Furthermore, the student's response may be used as a segue to a larger point the teacher wishes to make, possibly leaving the student with a residual feeling of distrust, anger, and discomfort.

Tiberuis and Flak offer useful steps to help reshape the learner-teacher alliance. This strategy requires, according to the authors, sharp and early detection of tension, arranging mutually friendly grounds for open but nonthreatening discussion, and actively listening with the intent to understand the context of a student's situation.

No classroom approach will prevent uncivil disruptions, but students today may feel the need to challenge in ways that perhaps earlier generations would not, with some exceptions in the 1960s. A recently retired community college CEO, upon returning to classroom teaching, remarked that the students do tend to engage—perhaps feeling they can enter and mentally withdraw from the classroom by their inattention, indifference, and their other-than-class preoccupations.

In an article in the fall 1998 issue of *College Student Affairs Journal*, Davis wrote that education leaders have not turned the corner on students' understanding of diversity. Her observations, based on works relating to race, gender, and sexual orientation, expose tension among students regarding their acceptance and understanding of these and related social issues. On data collected from the *Chronicle on Higher Education* from 1994 to 1997, 213 cases of incivility related to race, gender, and sexual orientation were published. In 76% of cases of campus tensions, students were the targets; in 17.8%, faculty members were targets; and in 6.5%, staff members were targets (p. 78). In addition, Davis points out that among the student cases, race was the dominant issue (84.3%). Among faculty cases, gender was the major predictor of tension (70.26%) (p. 80). According to Davis, all the categories of incidents appeared to be on the rise.

Balancing classroom inquiry and informed debate with an improved model of civility is a challenge. No model that education leaders might devise will be perfect, and if the model is too successful at curtailing incivility, the courts may strike it down. Perhaps the best hope is to maintain dialogue and strive for exemplary practices that are open for continual improvements. Judy Rookstool, a counselor at Evergreen Valley College in California, has examined civility policy in various schools and colleges. She has also looked at civility projects that operate out of universities such as Johns Hopkins and Rutgers. She cites these efforts as offering some promise, helping to guide teachers with the most effective practices towards creating ethical and civil environments, including the classroom.

University of California at Irvine Looks at Civility

The University of California at Irvine (UCI) started a newsletter to open a debate about faculty and administrative conduct. This newsletter allowed discussion of the climate that a responsible institution must engender. In "The Civility Debate: Defining the Problem, Exploring the Solutions," UCI Associate Dean of Arts Stephen Barker entered into a question-and-answer dialogue about the university's commitment to civility. The *UCI News'* questions and Barker's responses follow:

UCI News: *What does it mean to be civil?*
Barker: To be civil in the best sense is to seek mutual benefit from all interdependent interactions, to understand the positions of others before seeking to be understood, to value divergent opinions and perspectives—not merely to tolerate, let alone to condemn or overtly disrespect them. If one is not actively engaged in pursuing this model of civility—which includes a wide range of possibilities for disagreement, debate,

critical inquiry, dissent, and individuality—then one is actively engaged in subverting it. Further it is vital to remember that civility equals exchange. All civil exchange rests on a core of respect for the other, which means a decision not to assume power in an exchange but to understand the position of the other.

UCI News: *What are some of the forces influencing civility in academia today?*

Barker: Economic pressure, divergent political views, threats to tenure and thus to security, lack of public trust, growth of public cynicism, general "asocialism" of academics, and often fruitless efforts by academic units to emulate corporate models.

UCI News: *How are universities responding to the civility dilemma?*

Barker: Across the country, codes and rule structures attempting to right the listing ship of civility have begun to crop up. At Cornell, a new civility code contains the statement, "Faculty should avoid superficial and simplistic responses and engage in deeper consideration of the complex questions around us." This certainly seems reasonable, but the vague generality of the language seems to be in itself part of the shift from passionate confrontation that civility seems to entail. Today, the personal is political and academic.

UCI News: *What role should academia play in the civility debate?*

Barker: The university must be a model and a guide—not follow societal trends. We are not only the agents of social change but also its mentors. We must be better than the game we see around us. It is our job to galvanize attention but also to make sure that the content and presentation of what we do is exemplary. This is the challenge to administrators, faculty, and staff.

UCI News: *Is there a civility problem on this campus?*

Barker: Yes, at every academic level. Student to student, staff to student (and vice versa) and faculty to everyone. Each of these interchanges contains within it the danger of incivility, of inappropriate use of power relative to another. Even the administration is implicated in the problem: Students, staff, and faculty are always in danger of feeling out of touch with the unimportant in decisions made by central administration.

Consultation before decisions are made and feedback once decisions are made are vital to the well-being of any academic atmosphere. This obviously does not mean that all issues must be public ones, not that the will of a constituency needs to be followed. But it does mean that without consultation and feedback, no sense of trust and thus no nurturing of civility can occur.

UCI News: *How does language contribute to the problem?*

Barker: We in academia increasingly espouse the nomenclature of the business community—downsizing, efficiency, clients, customers, product, etc.—when in fact only through a gross oversimplification of the educational process at the university level can this analogy be made with more than a touch of validity. The university's values are quite different from those of a corporation, which means that academia is constantly not emulating a business model.

Of course, this is true at different intensities in different parts of this, or any, campus. Some disciplines lead more directly into the private sector than others; this negotiation is itself part of the civility of a campus.

UCI News: *Is the call for civility an impediment to the search for truth? If we were to give up incivility, would we also give up the ability to think for ourselves?*

Barker: Universities are beginning to respond to these questions. Responses range on campus from rules about speech—hate or otherwise—to codes of procedure that grow ever more complex. What, then, must be done? Not merely rules, if we are true to our academic ideals: Rules exist when teaching fails. We must demonstrate a world in which people maintain robust disagreements without turning them into ad hominem attacks or shallow and petty bickering, let alone violence. Even civil disobedience is a form of civility.

Perhaps, not surprisingly, the administration must actually lead this phalanx of groups in producing a civil atmosphere, even though administration is in constant danger of detachment, which leads to distrust and cynicism. This is true for chairs, deans, vice chancellors, chancellors, and even presidents.

UCI News: *What can we do to counteract this tendency toward detachment?*

Barker: Some strategies might include regular forums in which administrators and other constituencies confront issues together, open media interactions that supply information about events within the culture, open houses and town hall meetings to allow for debate, and overt and direct invitations for representatives of groups with views differing from the administrative policy to have access to administrators to discuss those views.

Additionally, there could be a campus-wide understanding about a "commitment to civility" disseminated to administrators, faculty, staff, and the surrounding community and stating the philosophy that civility—not a saccharine or lobotomized civility, but a boisterous and healthy one in which real debate can exist—is important to the campus.

UCI News: *Who should lead the way in this effort?*

Barker: Administration must be seen to lead in the area of civil openness and forthrightness or the atmosphere will not be created. This is one of the most difficult challenges administrators face—and the further up the administrative tree, the more difficult. The tone of civility on any campus comes from the top and can be significantly affected by strategies at the top administrative echelon, in each unit and campus-wide.

Our very survival as a meaningful organ of public debate may depend on our ability to devise and articulate conditions within which civil discourse can thrive (1997).

Barker's responses are important because they attempt to find the delicate balance between upholding the campus intellectual vitality and maintaining an acceptable civility. Barker cautions against creating a "benign and euthanized" academic environment. Learning, Barker asserts, requires the depth, the debate, and the pulls and tugs of inquiry and discovery, "not a saccharine or lobotomized civility, but a boisterous and healthy one in which real debate exists."

Barker believes that the entire climate of the campus must be set to uphold civility. He sees the leadership of the university as not only a change agent but also a mentor to the larger society. His view of mixing role responsibility is the animating principle of higher education—a deeply profound commitment to pushing the boundaries of inquiry, knowledge, spirit, and passion for learning.

Recommendations and Interventions for Employees

Many colleges have had a recalcitrant person who persistently attacked a colleague or an administrator or who aired complaints in an inappropriate forum. Eventually, such negative behavior may unfairly damage reputations and may even affect the health of persons and the whole organization. The CEO's role is central to creating and sustaining a healthy environment. Once a climate has deteriorated, the CEO has less opportunity to set forth a healthy climate for discussion and honest dissent, so the CEO should act earlier rather than later to set a strong example. Among the most important institutional factors are the CEO's presence and the CEO's position on civility. Consider these steps:

- The CEO sets and recognizes boundaries.
- The CEO is willing to say, "That is unacceptable."
- The CEO can recognize an unassailable principle when he or she sees it.
- The CEO listens to the environment so employees sense all three of the above points are true.
- The CEO is willing and able to model civility in his or her own behavior.
- The CEO is realistic enough to recognize that the CEO is also subject to errors in judgment and flexible enough to continually grow in order to improve effectiveness and capacity for leadership.

Institute Codes of Conduct

Many colleges have developed codes of conduct for employees. Teams of representative segments of the college should develop such codes, and outside assistance from legal services, counseling, or other expert communities should be brought into the discussion. Central Arizona College appears to have achieved such ownership through adoption of a code of conduct (see Appendix C).

A code of conduct can be a foundation for developing training packages with real case studies. One can assume that many employees often do not have a clear understanding of what constitutes inappropriate behavior. Central Arizona College cites its codes as helpful in setting higher behavioral standards. At a Mountain States Presidential retreat, former President John Klein stated that the following Central Arizona College Bill of Rights helped transform a highly toxic college environment to a healthy one (January 2001). He offered these tenets:

The Central Arizona College Bill of Rights
I.   All members of this community shall be free from
     a. intimidation

     b. retaliation

     c. abuse

     d. humiliation

     e. harassment

     f. interference that hinders the proper execution of their roles.

II. All members of this community ought to be entitled to

     a. due process

     b. adequate feedback and information to carry out their roles

     c. timely responses to requests and recommendations

     d. respectful consideration of their concerns

     e. the opportunity and responsibility for participation in the processes that determine the welfare of the community.

III. An ombudsperson at each campus will oversee the protection of these rights in coordination with the office of Human Resources (Central Arizona College, 2001).

Mention Civility in Employee Orientation

Civility is seldom introduced as a topic in an employee orientation session. The most important outcome of placing this topic in employee orientation is to instill ownership of this problem by everyone. Rick Miller, the former executive director of the Metropolitan Phoenix Boys and Girls Clubs and a Phoenix Think Tank participant, maintains that the most effective skill to teach children is the value of "being nice" (1999). Although it may sound simplistic, being nice is a powerful skill that in immense ways can minimize the woeful aspects of living.

Civility may even be an asset in negotiating and securing better life opportunities—a virtue that returns happiness, well-being, and success. When Kurt Landgraf was appointed as the new CEO of Educational Testing Services (ETS), he presented his staff with this quote from Benjamin Franklin, which he said guided his leadership code: "I will speak no ill of any man and speak all the good I know of everybody." Leaders, faculty, and staff in educational institutions could adopt such an attitude with positive results.

Institute Resolution Processes

Former Glendale Community College president John Waltrip spent a good part of his early career as a faculty leader and was responsible for writing the resident faculty policies (RFP) for the Maricopa Community College System in its formative years. Many of the protections, guarantees, and powers in the

RFP were incorporated before waves of future administrators and newer faculty came to Maricopa. The RFP could be considered a model compact. For example, it prohibited using more than 10% adjunct faculty in the day program, and faculty load and compensation were also spelled out. The RFP served all parties well at the Maricopa district, and grievances were infrequent. In fact, as chancellor at Maricopa, I went a couple of years without receiving a single grievance. The RFP provided mutually readable and clear guidelines for conduct, and it contributed to more stability than dissent.

Renew Passion for Education and Core Values

In the academic community, leaders may strain under the conventionally accepted code of objectivity, empiricism, and the scientific method. Even such important foundations of the academy as these do not let in the emotional, the subjective, and the intuitive processes that often really guide us through life. We may avoid allowing our emotional points of view and our passions contaminate the objective, but is it possible that those emotions and passions may also enhance our leadership?

The Spiritin' Group, a team of higher education specialists who promote authenticity and reexamination of higher education's core values, held a retreat in Malibu, California, in 2001, during which participants discussed aspects of American higher education. One point that emerged was the tendency of college and university presidents to "perfect the instrumentality and rationality" of their work, to the exclusion of the development of what one leader called "our interior." Although this group did not try to make the case that higher education was mean-spirited, it asserted that leaders and participants in higher education have become increasingly dispassionate, pragmatic, and externally driven.

Chickering (2003, pp. 39–44) has argued that higher education has begun to drift from the core beliefs of what a college education should do for the developmental stages of students. These beliefs would include ways in which colleges shape values and leaders' and students' responsibility as ethically based citizens. In contrast, Chickering asserted that education leaders have emphasized detached, cold empiricism and related methodologies that support science well but foster a depersonalization or dispassionate demeanor in our society. The competition in a market-centered world may lead to a tendency toward self-aggrandizement even in academe. Consideration for others and the civil commerce that we expect from people of good will become lost in the day-to-day setting.

Endorse the Employee Assistance Program

Most faculty and staff arrive at our colleges fully qualified, generally very positively disposed, earnest, and eager to do well, and they will most likely perform well for years to come. Leaders, however, often do not consider that staff members experience complex adult stages of development, including divorce, separation, or frustration with unfulfilled life goals. For example, on a survey of Maricopa employees, "frustrations and sense of failure of raising teenagers" was a frequently occurring impetus for seeking personal assistance through a creative employee assistance program (EAP). Other problematic conditions, such as substance abuse, often lead to deeper personal disorders.

It may be easier for troubled people whose life goals have been thwarted by advancing years, disillusionment, or dashed hopes to turn against peers, people in authority, and the institutions to which they owe their livelihood. People may come to work at a college when they are young, vigorous, and idealistic. If they later perceive they have missed opportunities or promotions, or if they finally just hit burn out, they may think they have little option but to lash out against the college, the policies, and the supposed motivations of the college leaders.

Faculty peers, administrators, and department chairs may tend to look the other way, neither setting boundaries nor issuing sanctions, but people who angrily lash out at others should not be ignored. An person whose behavior is destructive and inconsiderate is not necessarily an isolated person. Rather, a potential range of persons can be hurt by him or her—family, spouse, neighbors, colleagues, and whole communities. Cooling down a person's tension and stress can have wide-reaching effects on the general health of the academic community.

EAPs can help relieve stress in what are often the normal tensions of living; they also may help those who are operating under extraordinary stress. EAP may be shorthand for otherwise traditional counseling support that carries the negative undercurrent as treatment for mental illness—a type of illness that is still not accepted as legitimate in our society. A good EAP can help not only address anger management, but also provide help with family financial management, credit card abuse, alcohol and illegal and prescription drugs addictions, marriage and separation, difficulties of raising teenagers, and eating disorders.

Assistance with these issues is usually invisible, confidential, and almost always voluntary, yet people who represent the worse cases of abusive hostility are often not the ones who avail themselves of these services, mainly because such services could be considered treatment for mental illness. During the 1990s, Maricopa community colleges—a system that had more than 8,500 people on the payroll—went three years without top administrators placing a formal grievance on their chancellor's desk. EAPs had a role in that track record.

The theory behind EAPs is that most troubled staff or those in crisis can be helped by counseling, training, and personal support. The first consideration is to foster rehabilitation and personal support counseling before censure, discipline, or dismissal become the only options. Staff should have a trusted confidential method of accessing EAPs without the knowledge of the internal community or the CEO and the administration. EAPs may not always work, but they may assist colleges in avoiding painful sanctions and perhaps employee dismissals (Elsner, 2002).

Potential Results

All colleges have levels of dissonance on central academic and administrative issues. Healthy debate can cast light on difficult matters put before us, whereas unbridled, out-of-control anger can only add heat, not light, to matters at hand. Even a single person can inject divisive argument into a debatable issue; it is also possible to consider all sides of a debatable issue in an orderly and respectable manner. Leaders must be able to promote civil discourse. Assuming that well-thought-out codes of conduct are instituted and exemplified, and healthy interventions occur, community colleges could experience many potential benefits:

1. More conversations would occur.
2. Levels of creativity would rise.
3. People might live longer.
4. People would be healthier.
5. People would be happier.
6. Topics might be the same, but the interactions would be different.
7. Colleges would be seen as deriving a moral authority by our example—to be seen as objective, fair, caring, grounded for truth and responsibility.
8. Openness and safety on college campuses would increase.
9. A significant change in the chemistry of stress syndrome would occur:
    a. Decline of cardiovascular disease
    b. Decline of grievous conflicts
    c. Decline of substance abuse

10. Central motivation would be derived from passion for and caring of others.
11. Suppression of ego needs would be paramount.
12. More collaboration and less competition would be evident
13. A redefinition of power would occur:
    a. Power to interpret
    b. Power to listen
    c. Power of grace
    d. Power of synergy
    e. Power of freely developed human potential
    f. Power of peak experiences at high creativity
    g. The power of selflessness and the protecting of others needs

Conclusion

In some cases, existing campus environments may cause a student to drop out or cause an employee to become ill or to leave. College leaders may not be inclined to restrict people's behavior, language, or even their rage, and leaders and faculty members may not wish to speak much about inappropriate behavior. The contributors to this book hope to see this attitude change. We suggest that people should speak out against incivility and confront it when it occurs so that all those interested in the health of community colleges can help improve the climate of our institutions. We encourage community college leaders to seek a deeper understanding of the causes of campus incivility and to seek ways to foster and model an attitude of civility and civil discourse, both on campus and in the surrounding community.

References

Central Arizona College. (2001). *Policies and procedures.* Casa Grande, AZ: Author.

Chickering, W. A. (2003). Reclaiming our soul: Democracy and higher education. *Change*, January–February).

Davis, W. M. (1998). Toward civility: Assessment as a means toward improving campus climate. *College Student Affairs Journal, 18*(1).

Elsner, P. A. (2002). Comments before the Iowa State University Leadership Workshop, October 14.

Heinemann, R. L. (1996, November). *Addressing campus-wide communication incivility in the basic course: A case study.* Paper presented at the meeting of the SCA, San Diego, CA.

Kuhlenschmidt, S. L., & Layne, L. E. (1999, Spring). Strategies for dealing with difficult behavior. In *New directions for teaching and learning*. San Francisco: Jossey-Bass.

Peter, J. (2002, November). Offensive-speech ban weighed at Harvard; Critics look askance. *Arizona Republic*.

Tiberius, R. G., & Flak, E. (1999, Spring). Incivility in dyadic teaching and learning. In *New directions for teaching and learning*. San Francisco: Jossey-Bass.

University of California at Irvine Communications Office. (1997, April 9). *The civility debate: Defining the problem, exploring the solutions*. Irvine, CA: UC Regents. Available from http://www.communications.uci.edu/~inform

Appendix A:
AACC Model Code of Ethics for Community College CEOs

Preamble

The chief executive officers (CEOs of community, technical, and junior colleges set the ethical tone for their institutions through both their personal conduct and their institutional leadership.

Therefore, each CEO should adhere to the highest ethical standards and promote the moral development of the college community.

To achieve these goals, CEOs should support active moral reflection, dialogue and principled conduct among themselves, their boards of directors, administrators, faculty, staff, students, and the community at large.

While no code of ethics alone can guarantee ethical behavior, the values set forth in this code are intended to guide CEOs in carrying out these duties.

Values

To promote individual development and the common good, CEOs should strive to promote basic values about how people should conduct themselves when dealing with others in an academic institution serving the educational needs of the community. These values should represent a shared ideal which should permeate the institution and become for CEOs a primary responsibility to uphold and honor.

These values should include:
1. Trust and respect for all persons within and without the college.
2. Honesty inactions and utterances.
3. Fairness and justice in the treatment of all.
4. A pervasive sense of integrity and promise keeping.
5. A commitment:
    a. to intellectual and moral development
    b. to quality
    c. to individual empowerment
    d. to the community college philosophy
    e. to college above self.
6. Openness in communication.

7. Belief in diversity within an environment of collegiality and professionalism.

Responsibilites to Board Members

1. To ensure that all board members have equal access to complete information in a timely manner.
2. To avoid not only conflict of interest, but also the appearance of it.
3. To represent accurately positions of the board in public statements.
4. To foster teamwork and common purpose.
5. To carry out board policies in a conscientious and timely manner.

Responsibilites to Administration, Faculty and Staff

1. To encourage the highest standards of excellence in teaching and in the advancement and application of knowledge.
2. To respect both the personal integrity and professionalism of administrators, faculty, and staff.
3. To promote a college environment that fosters mutual support and open communication among all administrators, faculty, and staff.
4. To raise consciousness concerning ethical responsibilities and encourage acceptance of these responsibilities.
5. To seek and respect the advice of administration, faculty, and staff in matters pertaining to college life and governance.
6. To treat all employees fairly and equitably, to preserve confidentiality, to provide appropriate due process, and to allow adequate time for corrective actions.

Responsibilites to Students

1. To ensure that all students are treated with respect and to promote acceptance of diversity within the college community.
2. To provide quality education and equal access to educational opportunities for all students.
3. To provide accurate and complete descriptions of available academic programs and to provide sufficient resources to ensure viable programs.
4. To seek and respect contributions of students to college decisions.

5. To ensure that there is no unlawful discrimination, harassment, or exploitation in any aspect of student life.

Responsibilites to Other Institutions

1. To keep informed about developments at all levels of education particularly community, technical and junior colleges.
2. To be honest in reporting of college operations and needs.
3. To honor agreements and to maintain confidential information.
4. To respect the integrity of programs offered by other institutions and to promote collaboration.

Responsibilites to Business, Civic Groups, and the Community At Large

1. To ensure that the college responsibly meets changing needs in its state and communities.
2. To promise only what is realistic and keep promises that have been made.
3. To ensure that all interested parties have an opportunity to express their views regarding college policies.
4. To ensure equal opportunities or all groups to take part in college programs.
5. To avoid conflict of interest in contracts, services, or sharing of information.
6. To honor all laws pertaining to the college.

Rights of Chief Executive Officers

A CEO should have the right:
1. To work in a professional and supportive environment.
2. To a clear, written statement of the philosophy and goals of the college; to participate fully in setting subsequent goals and policies.
3. To a clear written statement of conditions of employment, board procedures for professional review, and a job description outlining duties and responsibilities.

4. Within the scope of authority and policy, to exercise judgment and perform duties without disruption or harassment.
5. To freedom of conscience and the right to refuse to engage in actions which violate professional standards of ethical or legal conduct.

Adopted April 1991

Appendix B:
Maricopa Office of General Counsel
Computing Resource Standards Statement

Introduction

The Maricopa County Community College District provides its students and employees wide access to information resources and technologies. With the advent of new forms of technology, Maricopa has recognized that the free exchange of opinions and ideas essential to academic freedom is furthered by making technological resources more accessible.

At Maricopa, technological resources are shared by its users; misuse of these resources by some users infringes upon the opportunities of all the rest. As Maricopa is a public institution of higher education, however, the proper use of those resources is all the more important. That Maricopa makes its technology available for educational purposes requires users to observe Constitutional and other legal mandates whose aim is to safeguard equipment, networks, data and software that are acquired and maintained with public funds.

General Responsibilities

Computing resources (including, but not limited to, desktop and laptop systems, printers, central computing facilities, District-wide or college-wide networks, local-area networks, access to the Internet, electronic mail and similar electronic information) of the Maricopa County Community College District are available only to authorized users, and any use of those resources is subject to these Standards. All users of Maricopa's computing resources are presumed to have read and understood the Standards. While the Standards govern use of computing resources District-wide, an individual community college or center may establish guidelines for computing resource usage which supplement (but do not replace or waive) these Standards.

Use of Maricopa's computing resources, including websites created by employees, is limited to educational, research, service, operational, and management purposes of the Maricopa County Community College District and its member institutions.

It is not Maricopa's practice to monitor the content of electronic mail transmissions, files, or other data maintained in its computing resources. The maintenance, operation and security of Maricopa's computing resources, however, require that network administrators and other authorized personnel have access to those resources and, on occasion, review the content of data and communications maintained there. A review may be performed exclusively by persons expressly authorized for such purpose and only for cause. To the extent possible in the electronic environment and in a public setting, a user's privacy will be honored. Nevertheless, that privacy is subject to Arizona's public records laws and other applicable state and federal laws, as well as policies of Maricopa's Governing Board--all of which may supersede a user's interests in maintaining privacy in information contained in Maricopa's computing resources.

Frequently, access to Maricopa's computing resources can be obtained only through use of a password known exclusively to the user. It is the user's responsibility to keep a password confidential. While Maricopa takes reasonable measures to ensure network security, it cannot be held accountable for unauthorized access to its computing resources by other users, within and outside the Maricopa community. Moreover, it cannot guarantee users protection against loss due to system failure, fire, etc.

Much of the data contained in Maricopa records that are accessible through use of computing resources is confidential under state and federal law. That a user may have the technical capability to access confidential records does not necessarily mean that such access is authorized. A user of Maricopa's computing resources is prohibited from the unauthorized access to, or dissemination of, confidential records.

Maricopa personnel are discouraged from offering advice to Maricopa employees regarding personal, non-job-related use, maintenance or repair of any computer equipment or software that belongs to such employees. Maricopa can assume no responsibility for any result from such advice.

Violation of any provision of the Standards could result in immediate termination of a user's access to Maricopa's computing resources, as well as appropriate disciplinary action. A violation of the Standards should be reported immediately to the appropriate administrator.

Prohibited Conduct

The following is prohibited conduct in the use of Maricopa's computing resources:

1. Posting to the network, downloading or transporting any material that would constitute a violation of Maricopa County Community College District contracts.

2. Unauthorized attempts to monitor another user's password protected data or electronic communication, or delete another user's password protected data, electronic communications or software, without that person's permission.

3. Installing or running on any system a program that is intended to or is likely to result in eventual damage to a file or computer system.

4. Performing acts that would unfairly monopolize computing resources to the exclusion of other users, including (but not limited to) unauthorized installation of server system software.

5. Hosting a website through the use of Maricopa's computing resources without the use of "maricopa.edu" in its URL. If an institution owns additional domain names, those services should directly reroute visitors to a "maricopa.edu" domain and not host web pages directly.

6. Use of computing resources for non-Maricopa commercial purposes.

7. Use of software, graphics, photographs, or any other tangible form of expression that would violate or infringe any copyright or similar legally-recognized protection of intellectual property rights.

8. Activities that would constitute a violation of any policy of Maricopa's Governing Board, including (but not limited to) Maricopa's non-discrimination policy and its policy against sexual harassment.

9. Transmitting, storing, or receiving data, or otherwise using computing resources in a manner that would constitute a violation of state or federal law, including (but not limited to) obscenity, defamation, threats, harassment, and theft.

10. Attempting to gain unauthorized access to a remote network or remote computer system.

11. Exploiting any computing resources system by attempting to prevent or circumvent access, or using unauthorized data protection schemes.

12. Performing any act that would disrupt normal operations of computers, workstations, terminals, peripherals, or networks.

13. Using computing resources in such a way as to wrongfully hide the identity of the user or pose as another person.

Faculty, Staff and Student Personal Website Standards

Faculty, staff and students may use Maricopa's computing resources for development of personal websites as a learning tool. Use of Maricopa's resources for this purpose is a privilege, not a right. The development and maintenance of such a website is subject to the following Faculty, Staff and Student Personal Website Standards, as well as the General Standards for Use of Maricopa's Computing Resources:

1. The author of a website may not use the site to advertise personal services, whether or not for financial gain, nor for any commercial purpose.

2. A website may not be created in such a way as to allow any person unauthorized access to Maricopa's computing resources.

3. The author of a website is solely responsible for the contents of the site. The home page of a personal website must display, or link to, the following disclaimer in a conspicuous manner: "This site is authored and maintained by [name of author]. It is not an official website of the Maricopa County Community College District, and Maricopa is not responsible for the contents of this site."

4. Maricopa does not endorse the contents of any personal website. It is solely the author's responsibility to ensure that the personal website comply with all relevant Standards, as well as state and federal law, and any relevant policy of Maricopa's Governing Board.

5. Upon discovery of a violation of any relevant Standard, Maricopa may unilaterally delete a personal website from its computing resources and terminate the author's access to those resources.

Appendix C:
Central Arizona College Code of Conduct

A Declaration of Civility for a Learning College

We affirm that all members of a learning college ought to be held in mutual respect; that they aspire to achieve and belong as do all people regardless of their title, job classification, or degree; that all members of the CAC community—student and teacher, manager and employee—are engaged in a common endeavor: the creation of an environment dedicated to learning.

We further affirm that the vitality of a learning college depends on a community where dialogues are honest and civil, where tough questions are raised and we can disagree without being disagreeable. Thus, it is the duty of every member of their community to actively and consciously help make this possible, committing each of us to personally uphold the virtues that lead to such a culture and to hold others accountable as well, privately and publicly. We should all be role models and hold each other to a consistent standard.

To achieve these ends, a behavior, which we shall call civility, must not only be practiced but form the basis for a new era of respect and trust among the members of this community. For without this civility—this respect and trust—the goal of becoming a place where learning is cherished will never be achieved.

Civility as we understand it flows from these basic virtues:
1. Integrity, including
   Honesty
   Fairness
   Sincerity
2. Fidelity, including
   Faithfulness to the spirit of a learning college
   Allegiance to the public trust
3. Charity, including
   Kindness
   Caring
   Goodwill
   Tolerance
   Compassion

4. Responsibility, including
   Reliability
   Accountability
   Trustworthiness
5. Self-discipline, including
   Acting with reasonable restraint
   Not indulging in excessive behavior

Finally, we affirm that these virtues must be modeled first and foremost by those members who wear the mantle of leadership. It must be modeled foremost by the leaders within the student body, faculty, staff, and administration because it is to them that the rest of the community looks for direction, for support, and for wisdom in our common endeavor to make this a place of learning.

About the Contributors

George R. Boggs is president and chief executive officer of the American Association of Community Colleges (AACC) based in Washington, DC. AACC represents more than 1,100 associate degree-granting institutions and more than 11 million students. Boggs previously served as faculty member, division chair, and associate dean of instruction at Butte College in California, and for 15 years he served as the superintendent/president of Palomar College in California. He served as a member of the Committee on Undergraduate Science Education of the National Research Council and has served on several National Science Foundation panels and committees. He holds a bachelor's degree in chemistry from The Ohio State University, a master's degree in chemistry from the University of California at Santa Barbara, and a PhD in educational administration from The University of Texas at Austin.

Paul A. Elsner spent nearly a decade in the Peralta Community College District in California during the periods following the "free speech" movement of the 1960s and the assassinations of Martin Luther King, Jr. and John F. Kennedy. His tenure saw the rising of resistance to the Vietnam War. Following his work at Peralta, Elsner served for 22 years as chancellor at the Maricopa County Community College District in Arizona—now the largest community college district in the United States. He is also president and founder of the Sedona Conferences and Conversations, an international forum that examines social as well as technological issues.

Zelema Harris is the president of Parkland College, located in Champaign, Illinois. She has been a community college president for 24 years, 14 of those as CEO. She has taught at the high school and college level, and she is a frequent speaker on topics of teaching and learning leadership, diversity, and planning. She is a visiting faculty member in the Community College Leadership Program at Austin, Texas, and AACC's Future Leaders Institute.

Martha Gandert Romero serves as founding director of the Community College Leadership Development Initiatives. Nationally, she has been a consultant to businesses and industries, foundations, and institutions of higher education such as the Arizona State University Continuing Education Division, University of Colorado School of Education, the Institute for

Educational Leadership's Education Policy Fellowship Program, University of New Mexico Community College's Leadership Program, University of Alaska System, the League for Innovation Executive Leadership Institute, the National Bureau of Standards, Boulder County Mental Health Center, and the YWCA. She has established programs for leadership development in a variety of settings.

Judy Rookstool has served in a number of faculty and administrative positions within the San Jose/Evergreen Community College (SJECC) District since 1976. An academic and personal counselor for much of her career, she has taught in developmental English and student guidance. She has served as director of school and community relations and director of student activities. During a sabbatical leave, she developed a body of knowledge on civility in the classroom, and has spoken widely on the topic. She received a SJECC District Carnegie Scholar Award, which allowed her to complete a classroom action research project on teaching civility in the classroom.

Rookstool holds a bachelor's degree in sociology from the University of California, Santa Barbara, a master's degree in counselor education from San Jose State University, and an EdD in organization and leadership from the University of San Francisco. Currently she is the coordinator of the teaching and learning at Evergreen Valley College.

Beverly S. Simone served as president of Madison Area Technical College. She is one of the few women in the nation who has led a public two-year multicampus college reporting directly to a governing board. Simone's background includes 30 years as a teacher and administrator in community, vocational, and technical colleges, as well as significant experience as a businessperson and entrepreneur in Indianapolis, Indiana. In addition, she consulted with industries, including IBM, Blue Cross/Blue Shield, and Indiana National Bank, in management and organizational communication. She has received recognition nationally and internationally for her vision and abilities.

Index

administration, 32, 39, 69–70
    responsibilities to, 80
administrative reorganizations, 6
American Association of Community Colleges (AACC), 1
    model code of ethics for community college CEOs, 10, 79–82
"angry faculty letter" incident, 53
Argyris, C., 38
Association of Community College Trustees, 10
authority, resistance to, 4–5

Barker, Stephen, 67–70
Berkeley, California, 19–20. *See also* Northern California community
    colleges in late 1960s
Black community, 49–51
Black Panthers, 13, 14, 18, 19
Black power and Black liberation movements, 13, 14, 16, 18–19
board members
    bad behavior among, 9
    responsibilities to, 80
board of trustees, 7, 35–37
    conflicts among, 61–62
boardroom, as arena for clash of values, 27–31
Boyer, Ernest, 11
business, responsibilities to, 81

California. *See* Northern California community colleges in late 1960s
Carter, S. L., 54
censure, fear of, 63
Central Arizona College
    Bill of Rights, 71–72
    Code of Conduct, 87–88
chairs. *See also* boardroom
    department, 5
Chickering, W. A., 73
chief executive officers (CEOs), 4, 7–10, 31, 32, 60. *See also* under
    American Association of Community Colleges
    absence, 63